C'EST LA GUERRE

THE MEMOIR OF CAPT. JAMES MCBRAYER SELLERS, USMC

WILLIAM SELLERS   JAMES GREGORY

STEVEN GIRARD

Gray Sparrow
BOOKS

Published by Gray Sparrow Books, an imprint of Storied Publishing

Copyright ©2020 James Gregory

Permission requests and other questions may be directed to the Contact page at www.storied.pub.

ISBN: 978-1-951991-07-4

Cover design by Sean Benesh

Colorizations by Lewis Hayes Jr.

This work is dedicated to all the men who served with the 4th Brigade (Marine), 2nd Division, AEF, and to those who gave the "Last Full Measure of Devotion" and forever lay in the green fields of France. Semper Fidelis.

To MSG Michael D. Girard, USA, Ret. Former Corporal, United States Marine Corps, 1st and 3rd Marine Divisions, Republic of Vietnam, August, 1964 to November 1966.
Miss you dad. ASNF.

To Anna and all my "girls"—thanks for the love and support, I'm always proud of you.

Steven Girard

CONTENTS

.

PREFACE

This story comes from the mind of a great hero of the First World War, Capt. James McBrayer Sellers, USMC. He retold his experiences to his son, also named James Sellers, in oral interviews in the late 1980s. These interviews were taped and transcribed into a memoir, which the elder James Sellers proofread and corrected. After Sellers Sr. passed away in September of 1990, his family found a stash of unknown letters that he had written during the war. William W. Sellers, the grandson of James Sellers Sr., took it upon himself to combine the letters into the already existing memoir. James P. Gregory Jr. and Steven C. Girard then edited the manuscript into its final form. The memoir now contains all of the identifying information for names mentioned to ensure future historians have no trouble with the references. Certain details about locations and engagements have also been added in to give a fuller understanding of Capt. Sellers' memoir.

Capt. Sellers' account of his time during the war is a fantastic look from enlistment to the discharge of a U.S. Marine Corps officer during the First World War. Starting at his enlistment and then training at Winthrop and Quantico, to the battlefields of France, the Occupation of Germany, and eventual settling after the war, this account illuminates a new perspective in Marine Corps history. His unique position within the corps gave him more information during his service than regular enlisted men. This is shown through his letters that were slipped passed the censor, since he himself did the censoring of his company, and gave more information to his family in the states. He also kept track of locations and dates, as seen in the appendix. These, paired with his near perfect memory, create a very detailed and interesting account.

INTRODUCTION

JAMES MCBRAYER SELLERS

James Mcbrayer Sellers, the youngest of five children to Sandford and Lucia Sellers, was born on June 20, 1895 in the Sellers' family quarters on the second floor of Wentworth Military Academy's administration building in Lexington, Missouri. Except for the period from 1912 to 1920, when he was at the University of Chicago and in the Marine Corps, he spent his entire life at Wentworth. His career was extraordinary in its longevity and productivity. He served the Academy as its Superintendent for 27 years, as President for 52 years, and as a teacher for 70 years. As with many who have careers in education, his life is better defined by the lives he touched and affected than by his own actions.

Wentworth Academy was founded by Stephen G. Wentworth in 1880. To run the school, he hired a 21 year-old schoolmaster, Benjamin Hobson. Hobson recommended that Wentworth also hire Sandford Sellers, one of Hobson's old classmates from Centre College in Danville. Sandford Sellers joined his old schoolmate at Lexington in the summer of 1880. While Hobson left Wentworth after one year to prepare for the ministry, Sandford Sellers stayed on for 58 years, serving variously as principal, superintendent, owner, and president.

Wentworth enrolled 37 students during the first term, but the Academy was able to build upon those modest beginnings. The school added a military regimen to the course of instruction in 1882, and in 1890, the name was changed to Wentworth Military Academy. By that time Wentworth had become a regional institution with 113 cadets from 6 states. The War Department first stationed a Professor of Military Science at Wentworth in 1896. The state of Missouri conferred the rank of Major upon Sandford Sellers in 1893 and that of Colonel in 1899.

Sandford married Lucia Valentine Rogers of Waco, Texas, in 1882. The Sellers had five children: Ovid (1884), Marcia (1886), Pauline (1889), Sandford Jr. (1892), and James McBrayer (1895). Young "McBrayer," as he was called as a boy, and his siblings had the run of the school grounds in their youth. He started school at the Lexington Ladies College under the tutelage of "Miss Lutie" Chambers in 1903. He was the only one who entered that year so he was in a class by himself.

In 1906, Miss Lutie's school closed, and he entered seventh grade in the Lexington public school. The next year, he entered high school at Wentworth. While there, McBrayer participated in a wide variety of activities. He was a member of the cavalry unit and the rifle team that won the national scholastic championship, while he himself won the Burnap Trophy for indoor rifle marksmanship. He excelled in his studies and won the scholastic gold medal. He lettered in football in the fall, basketball in the winter, and track and tennis in the summer, winning the silver cup in tennis. After completing four years of high school, his oldest brother Ovid, who had returned to become the dean of students at Wentworth, persuaded McBrayer to remain an additional year at Wentworth, since he was only 15 at graduation in 1911. In that extra year, Mac had a one-man Greek class with Ovid as his instructor, and they played a game of chess to see whether he would earn a 90 or a 95. He got a 95.

Because of the school's high academic record, Wentworth graduates at the time were allowed entrance without examination to the country's best universities, including West Point and Annapolis. In the fall of 1912 McBrayer chose to follow his older brothers to the University of Chicago. At that time, a Bachelor of Arts degree could only be earned by a student whose major was the Classics. No Greek credit appeared on his Wentworth transcript, so as a freshmen, he enrolled in Greek 1. With a full year of undisclosed instruction behind him, he appeared to be a young genius and his reputation was made in the Classics Department. He also had a major in geology and a minor in mathematics.

At the end of his freshman year, he came down with a virus that necessitated his coming home to recuperate. He did not return to Chicago for the 1913-1914 school year, instead remaining at Wentworth where he taught an English class, coached the rifle team, and ran the school store called the Quartermaster.

McBrayer returned to the University of Chicago in the fall of 1914 and immersed himself in the collegiate atmosphere. He spent the falls of 1914, 1915, and 1916 on the football team. He was a member of Sigma Xi and the Beta Theta Pi fraternity. At the beginning of his senior year, he was elected one of twelve University Marshalls, and was called upon to assist at various University functions, sometimes riding on horseback in a suit of armor. He graduated in absentia in 1917 due to the war.

James McBrayer Sellers entered the United States Marine Corps in April of 1917 and was commissioned as a second lieutenant. During the First World War, he participated in the battles of Belleau Wood, Blanc Mont Ridge, and the Meuse-Argonne Offensive, and was in command of the 78th Company, 2nd Battalion, 6th Regiment for the latter two battles. For bravery in action, he was awarded the Distinguished Service Cross, the Navy Cross, the Silver Star Medal, the Purple Heart

Medal, and the French Croix-de-Guerre. Discharged from active service in 1920, he remained in the Marines as a reserve officer until his honorary retirement in 1944 with the rank of lieutenant colonel.

In the spring of 1920, McBrayer returned to Wentworth. In 1923, Wentworth expanded its student base by adding a Junior College, which would soon account for half the student population. From 1922 to 1928, "Major Mac," as he was affectionately known by the cadets of the era, was Commandant in charge of the daily activities and discipline at the school. He also taught Latin, mathematics, and English and coached intramural football and tennis.

In 1925, McBrayer began dating a young woman from Independence, Missouri by name of Rebekah Hall Evans (1901-1985). She was the great-granddaughter of Academy founder Stephen G. Wentworth and a Phi Beta Kappa graduate of Smith College. They were married on December 20, 1925 and had three children, Stephen Wentworth (1926), James McBrayer Jr. (1929), and Fred Evans (1941). The family lived in an apartment in the second floor of the Administration Building.

During the Depression in the early 1930s, enrollment at Wentworth plummeted to such an extent that with overhanging debts and diminishing income, it was necessary for either Sandy or James to depart. James was able to borrow some money from his father-in-law, and bought out his brother's third interest in the school and became the Superintendent in 1933, after having served five years as Executive Officer. Shortly thereafter, Lester Wikoff bought Sandford Sellers Sr.'s third interest and the two ran the school together until Wikoff's retirement in 1971. The private ownership of the Academy ceased in 1951 when it was re-incorporated as a nonprofit organization.

In the 1920s, James Sellers began a long friendship with Harry and Bess Truman. James and Harry were able to get acquainted with each other through their mutual Masonic affiliation. Rebekah Sellers had been a classmate of Bess's younger brother, Fred Wallace, while growing up in Independence, so she had known Bess as a girl in the early years of the century. Harry made a few trips to Lexington to visit the town and address the Wentworth cadet corps as he was climbing the political ladder from Jackson County Judge to United States Senator to Vice-President and finally President of the United States. After the Truman's return to Independence in 1953, James and Rebekah entertained them at the their new home, Sunset View, built in 1952 and situated on the bluffs overlooking the Missouri River. During the Founder's Day celebration honoring the 75th anniversary of Wentworth in 1954, Truman laid wreaths on the graves of Sandford Sellers and Stephen G. Wentworth and delivered an address on the Cold War to the cadet corps. Harry presented James with his ten-page speech which he had written by hand on a Big Chief tablet, and Mac, in turn, made Harry S. Truman an "Honorary Colonel" in the Wentworth cadet corps.

Shortly after World War II broke out in 1941, James Sellers returned to active duty in the Marine Corps. While attending the American Military Schools and Colleges meeting in Washington, D.C., in early 1942, James met with General Thomas E. Holcomb, his Battalion Commander in the First World War who had risen to the position of Commandant of the Marine Corps. General Holcomb told him that he could do the country much more good by preparing young men for the service at Wentworth and asked him to stay in the Marine Reserves but continue his work in Lexington. During World War II, Wentworth's enrollment reached record heights and school continued year round so young men could join the service with military experience and a diploma in hand.

In the summer of 1950 following a three-set tennis match, McBrayer suffered a major heart attack which curtailed his activities for a while, but he recovered sufficiently to ready the school for the fall opening. Shortly after his heart attack, Sellers received the following handwritten letter from the Marine Corps Commandant: "30 Aug. 1950. Dear Sandy: I have just received word of your recent attack so I'm rushing a note of good cheer from your Marine Corps friends and to wish you a speedy recovery. Here is hoping you are back on the court by the time this arrives—but, remember this is not 1918, so we must accept the fact that we have to take it a little easier. My very best to you and yours. As ever, Clif Cates."

He also began moving up in the state Masonic organization, in which he had been active for some time. In 1951-52, he served as Grand Commander of the Grand Commandery of Missouri and in 1953-54 was Grand Master, the highest state Masonic office. He was involved in other local and national activities throughout his life. He was an elder of the Presbyterian Church of Lexington. In the 1930s he was involved in the Goose Pond Minstrels, a group of local citizens who put on a variety show to raise money for local parks and activities. He usually performed as an "end man," where his duty was to sing an original pianologue insulting as many prominent members of the community as possible. He often made appearances on radio and television programs and was never hesitant in writing editorial letters to the Kansas City Star on issues of import when he was concerned over the state of the country.

With Wentworth on solid ground in 1960, James Sellers stepped down as superintendent, turning the reins over to his longtime partner, Colonel Lester Wikoff. Sellers remained at the school as president and chairman of the board, and daily went to his office, located directly under the room in which he was born, to teach Latin. Wentworth's enrollment again reached record heights during the Vietnam conflict in the 1960s, but in the early 1970s, the backlash against the military as a result of Vietnam caused enrollment to drop precipitously. Seller's son, James McBrayer Sellers, Jr., returned to Wentworth as Superintendent in 1973, and Sellers Sr. was able to help him stabilize the Academy while many similar institutions closed their doors throughout the country. By 1980 enrollment was again on an upswing, During the 1970s and 1980s Mac taught Latin to all six of his male grandchildren and continued his routine of teaching and guiding students through the 1989-90 school year.

Lieutenant Colonel James McBrayer Sellers passed away on September 5, 1990, at the age of 95. During his long and productive tenure at Wentworth, he inspired thousands of graduates to successful military and civilian careers. James McBrayer Sellers and Wentworth Military Academy are synonymous; one cannot be thought of without the other.

1

ENLISTMENT

After Christmas of 1916, the war clouds were gathering and I became very restive. I had a hard time studying and doing my usual chores. During my senior year at the University of Chicago, war was declared against Germany and the other Central Powers. Shortly after the American Declaration of War on April 6, 1917, I received a letter from my brother Sandy, who was then an administrator at Wentworth Military Academy in Lexington, Missouri. He wrote that the Marine Corps would commission 10 Wentworth graduates on nothing but the recommendation of the Academy, since it was one of the nation's designated honor schools. This privilege was also granted to a number of our finer universities.

The Marine Corps had not been widely publicized in those days, and I was not familiar with them. Believe it or not, I didn't know what the Marine Corps was. I had a vague idea that it was something like the Coast Guard or the Merchant Marine. Before burning any of my bridges by dropping out of my classes, I made a trip down to the recruiting office in Chicago to inquire about being fit and the possibility of getting a Marine commission. There were five other university men down there also, so I felt that I'd have good company. There were thirteen being examined when Doc Wiley, a Phi Gam, and I hit the place. Finally one of the fellows came out and reported that only three out of the bunch had passed. I almost gave up hope then. But I thought I'd better stick it out. One of the fellows who failed was "Red" Jackson, captain of the university football team of that year. He and I had played football for Amos Alonzo Stagg's team at Chicago. Seven young fellows were in our crowd. Red was our captain the previous fall, and he always became extremely excited and agitated before a game. He was in a similar state before the physical, and his heart rate was so rapid that he failed. I was able to calm him down, and he passed his second exam.

On the first test, for color blindness, everyone passed. Then on the next test the first fellow came through with flying colors. The applicant was placed twenty feet away from a card on which letters are printed. If he could read the letters with one eye he was scored twenty. If he could not read them, he was moved up a foot. Then if he could read, he was scored a nineteen. A score of nineteen and twenty was required of a candidate. Well, the next fellow got sixteen and fourteen. Then Doc Wiley came up, and he had to be moved up to ten feet on one eye and eight feet on the other. Five of the original seven failed on this test. I came last, and, rather to my surprise, I got twenty-twenty. Thus there were only two left. The other fellow then was found to be 5 feet 4 inches in height. So I was left alone. The doc finally passed me without a question.

The recruiters gave me a big song and dance, but I was sold anyway. So I went back to school and told my dean, Teddy Linn, about my opportunity. The Dean told me to go ahead and join and he would make sure that I received my diploma. I got credit for my last quarter's work, and my degree was given to me "*in absentia.*" Thus I entered the Marine Corps in April of 1917, never really finishing the school year. I immediately wrote my parents, hoping and supposing that they approved of my decision. The action was not binding except for three

2

months, and after that, if I renewed my commission, until the war was over. I did hate to leave college, because the spring quarter in a man's senior year is supposed to be the high spot in his whole career. But a great many of my friends were leaving for one sort of service or another, and I felt that I ought to do my duty to my country also.

In retrospect I never cease to marvel at my mother's attitude. When as youngsters we used to go down to the river almost every day during the summer, paddle our canoe and swim, she never worried but took the attitude that her sons had sense enough not to drown themselves. She exhibited the same reaction when I came home and told her that I was joining the Marine Corps.

A lieutenant told me that a stiff course of training would be waiting for us with lots of drilling and studying of Marine regulations. He assumed, and he was right, that I would thoroughly enjoy getting back into the old harness and marching around to the call of bugles. We expected to get very intensive training which would fit us in a minimum of time for duty. I thought that the Marine Corps was just the thing for me. Besides, as soon as I took the oath, my pay amounting to $140 a month would begin, which was more than I could make at anything else.

In May, I left home to report for duty. The trip was uneventful until I arrived in Chicago, where I was to be sworn in. Upon arrival I went out to the University, greeted all the fellows who were left, passed on the news from Lexington to my brother Ovid, and then went down to catch a train for a house-party the girls from the Wyvern Club were putting on at Twin Lakes. Only the men were on the train and we played cards and fooled around till our arrival. The girls met us at the train and took us over to the hotel in a motorboat.

The surroundings were ideal for such a party; two lakes and plenty of boats, and a roughly furnished hotel. We dined, rowed around on the lakes, sang, and performed on our ukeleles until eight o'clock, then retired to the hotel for a dance. The young lady with whom I was fortunate enough to be paired was an excellent dancer, so I enjoyed the proceedings considerably. After the dance we sat around and sang for an hour, then retired. Most of the fellows had so much pep though, that I did not finally compose myself in the arms of Morpheus until about five o'clock in the morning. We arose the next morning for breakfast to find the beautiful weather departed. A cold wind had blown up, and we had to take violent exercise playing baseball and run sheep run to keep warm. A big wood fire in the hotel parlor attracted most of the crowd, and we all performed according to our ability. I sang my usual repertoire of blues and my specialty song, "Ivan Petrovsky Spivar" In the afternoon the sun came out again; so my girl and I took a long walk around the lake. We had more music after dinner and I did not retire until about 1:00 a.m. I had to leave early Monday morning in order to get back by 10:00 a.m. for my exam.

The headquarters where our examiners were entrenched was way up on the tenth floor of a ratty looking building in Chicago. There were about 55 or 60 fellows who were there to take the examination, and I soon found five fellows from the university who were also taking it. My Wentworth classmates and fellow Lexingtonians Mordecai Chambers and William Wallace Ashurst were also on the train. We three men from Wentworth were about twenty-fifth on the list, so our examination didn't come until 2:30. Mordecai got in first, and they gave him a card with a number to take down to the final board. Ashurst and I went in together. Two doctors tapped us all over and gave us cards with numbers also. By the time we came out, Mordecai had returned from the caucus below and said that he had failed the physical examination. He was rather broken up about it, especially because he didn't know what his failing was.

Ashurst and I then went down, and we were ushered in to an imposing trio of old officers. They said we had passed the physical exam, then looked over our papers, shot us a little hot air about what a fine organization we were applying for admission to, and told us to report to another office to be sworn in at 4:30. We were sworn in as 2nd lieutenants in the reserve corps then. It seemed that we had to be sworn in before we would receive our final commission from the President. The officers didn't seem to know when we would be ordered out, but said that probably we should have to wait for some four to six weeks. These delays were certainly discouraging, when all of us were so anxious to get down to business. I had all this time on my hands and had nothing particular to do.

Mordecai finally got an interview with his inspector, and found that his heart was bad. The doc said that perhaps the cause was fatigue from the recent traveling, and that if he came back the next morning he could pass possibly. He eventually passed his physical and received his Marine commission. Ashurst and I made a trip home to Lexington to await the call, which we received in mid-June of 1917.

After Wallace Ashurst and I left the train depot at Higginsville, Missouri we had an uneventful trip to St. Louis. At St. Louis we met a couple of other Marine officers—one from Western Military Academy who lived in southern Missouri. We caught a B&O train out of St. Louis for Philadelphia, and it was just our luck that it ran five and a half hours late before we got to Philadelphia. The scenery on our trip was lost on us, because we were covered with dust and roasted too. However I did enjoy winding in and out among the mountains of West Virginia. I met an old Beta on the train. He was a native of Philadelphia and before we got there, he explained the plan of the city to me. So we had no trouble finding a hotel for the night and the Quartermaster's Depot when we arrived at the Quaker City. We found that our supplies were very hard to get. The Depot was out of trunks and bedrolls—so at that time I had no luggage except what I left home with, nor any bedding.

We stayed in Philadelphia Thursday night and Friday,

getting as much as we could of our supplies and left for Washington D.C. Friday night. At Washington, we continued our search for more uniforms and finally got it all ordered without much chance of getting it for some time. At 2:05 we started on the last leg of our trip and arrived at a camp called Indian Head, a temporary bivouac camp at Winthrop, Maryland, just upstream from Washington, D.C.

2

WINTHROP

The Winthrop camp was nothing but a rifle range surrounded by a few shacks and hundreds of tents. Most of the fellows had been there a couple of days and had the good quarters cabbaged. But luckily I found an overlooked cot in the best shack, so I was fixed up pretty well, though I didn't have any bedding except a couple of sheets. The fellows there were in general a fine bunch gathered in from Maine to Butte, Montana. For three weeks my friend Wallace Ashurst and I did nothing but practice marksmanship. It turned out that we were the only two who qualified on the Naval course. The Marine lieutenant colonel who was in charge of our group had been informed that the Marines were to change from the traditional Navy drill manual to the Army drill manual. The Army foot and rifle movements were totally different from the Navy movements, and the lieutenant colonel knew nothing about them, so he did not teach them.

Instead, we did nothing but practice marksmanship for three weeks, firing the M1903 Springfield .30 caliber rifle. Meanwhile we received our first taste of shell-fire. Down the river from us, they were testing some big guns, and their point of aim was the water tank about twenty yards from our shack. We were being instructed in grenade throwing at the time they started firing. Of course, they aimed to shoot over the shack, but we all cleared out when they started. The previous year, so the rumor went, when engaged in a similar occupation, they demolished our kitchen.

Winthrop had no civilian population whatsoever. It consisted of a bevy of tents, three barrack shacks, a frame building used as headquarters, and a post exchange, where the enlisted men loafed and bought ice cream and tobacco. Immediately behind us stretched the rifle range, 1000 yards long. The post was used only for rifle practice, and the different Marine companies were arriving there one at a time for instruction in shooting.

There was no drilling at all for us. The Marine drill regulations were different from the old army regulations, so the commanding officer started in the first week to give us instruction. But as soon as we began making a little headway, word was received from headquarters that the army regulations were to be adapted for us for the period of the war. So since most of us had had experience in Infantry drill, we had been devoting our time simply to our rifles, pistols, grenades, and machine guns. We had to learn how to take all these apart and put them back together.

Reserve officers had been coming in a few at a time ever since we had arrived there, until we numbered about 88. We were under the command of a young Annapolis graduate who had recently received his appointment as 2ndLt. in the Marines. We were under the direction of the commanding officer, Col. George Croghan Reid, USMC, who assigned us our duties for each day. Every one of us had to become thoroughly acquainted with range work. My first day, I went into the butts and pulled targets during the morning, then shot the preliminary course in the afternoon. All of us took turns pulling targets and supervising recruits as they pulled them. There were different targets to be fired at on different ranges, and in rapid fire we had to hold the targets up a certain length of time. William W. Ashurst and I had found our training on the range at Wentworth rather valuable here. We led the field with our scores on the range, and I was in hopes we would make good scores when we shot for record. It was a good deal a matter of luck as to whether we would make good records, because so much depends on the weather.

We were right on the Potomac River, upstream, far enough, not to have any waves, and only about two feet of tide, but far enough downstream so that there was practically no current in it. This was the scene, so they told me, of a good deal of naval activity during the Civil War. The river was about three or four miles wide, rather deep and as placid as a lake. Big excursion boats, tugs, and sail boats plied it daily, and there was a regular boat line between Norfolk and Washington which passed by us. One night, when I was calling on Col. and Mrs. Reid, a trim little yacht passed by us going toward Washington. Mrs. Reid jumped up, seized her field glasses and announced that the Russian Embassy and Secretary of the Navy Josephus Daniels were taking a little pleasure excursion. That same boat was used by President Wilson when he needed some fresh air.

Our only regular officers here were Col. Reid, a fine youngish old fellow Capt. Woolman G. Emory, USMC, post Quartermaster, and Lieutenants Roy C. Swink, USMC, and Frank Z. Becker, USMC. The latter was a recently promoted man from the ranks, a man on the order of Wentworth's Sergeant Blue, only younger. He instructed us in the use of the rifle, and was the permanent range officer at the post. Officers were so shy, or rather scarce, that the several hundred enlisted men at this post were under the command of enlisted men. Everything was exceedingly informal there, because of the lack of female population. The enlisted men wore undershirts nearly all the time as the outer garment, and our uniform consisted only of a campaign hat, O.D. shirt and khaki trousers, without leggings. Everyone that was there, although busy, seemed to be on holiday. There were no long faces, and there was little talk of the war. We had baseball games and we went swimming and boat riding every day. In fact we were enjoying life intensely.

I was helping coach some new recruits in shooting and I found out that they were in a company which had been recruited in Minnesota. About 70 were from the university. They had been sent to Mare Island Navy Yard, Vallejo, California, in April 1917. Then two weeks before arriving at Winthrop they had been at Quantico, and from what they told me, I found out that we would not have such a picnic when we get there. They had been drilled six or seven hours a day, until many of them were fainting. They said the doctors had to call a halt on the work. I imagined, however, that we would not have such strenuous work.

At the time I was making a goodly number of friends in the bunch. Many of them were widely known athletes, and nearly all were quick to learn and capable. But of course there were a few misfits. In the conversation around the tables every variety of pronunciation was heard. A few had the Boston accent, some talked so that I could tell at once that they had come from Texas, others were westerners, and one or two were from Virginia or Maryland. They came from Yale and Minnesota, New Mexico Military Academy, and Western Military Academy. But everyone got along well, and we were happy.

At Winthrop's range we fired an Army course, shooting at one range 200 yards standing, 300 yards sitting, and 500 yards in the prone position in order to qualify as a marksman, a sharp shooter, or an expert. The M1903 Springfield was a very accurate weapon, and a number of us qualified as experts. We also fired the Navy course, which involved firing at different ranges —200 to 500 yards—for marksman, sharp shooter, and expert.

The expert course was fired at 500 yards, sitting, kneeling, and standing, part of it without post control. The Navy course was extremely difficult, particularly at 500 yards without the use of a post to steady oneself. Wallace Ashurst and I were the only ones to qualify as experts out of the 116 brand new second lieutenants in our group. Our Wentworth training obviously had held us in good stead. Ashurst served as a platoon leader in France during the war and later headed the Marine Corps rifle training. He won the Individual National Rifle Marksman Championship in 1924 at Camp Perry, Ohio.

Of the various Navy qualification courses, on the marksman I did not do particularly well, but I was among the highest five. The marksman course was a very complicated affair. We shot ten shots prone, five slow and five rapid fire, and repeated the performance kneeling, squatting, and standing. Then we shot the changing position fire, where the target would come up for five seconds and we shot one shot prone at it; then it went down for five seconds, came up and we shot one shot from the kneeling position, then one squatting, one more kneeling and one more prone. We repeated the whole performance four times. The Navy expert course was the same as the marksman course but it was shot at five hundred yards. To qualify one had to make 210 out of the possible 300. Otherwise, one had to make 70 in the changing position shooting. About 75 fellows shot the afternoon I did; we were divided into relays, and 16 shot at the same time. 500 yards was supposed to be the most difficult range of all to fire on, because it was the longest range fired without rest, or artificial support. I didn't expect to do much therefore. On the slow fire I got 83 out of a possible 100. My next competitor got 81. Then in the rapid fire I got 78, and all the other fellows who had done anything at slow fire fell down here. I needed only 49 in the changing positions to qualify and all the others needed 70. One man made an even seventy and qualified, although his total was about 150. I shot in the last relay, and when it came our turn a big rain started pouring down on us. We were allowed to shoot with the peep sight, which is much more accurate than the open, and I was trying to use it in the rain. Pretty soon though I saw that with a big drop of water in the peep I wouldn't have much chance; so I threw my sight down and used the battle sight. I succeeded in making 58 in spite of the rain and qualified with a total of 219. Besides the other fellow who made 70, I was the only one to qualify. I talked to my coach, an enlisted man who was stationed there permanently as a coach, and he said that he had failed on the Navy expert course the week before, so I felt pretty chesty about the whole affair.

I became quite fascinated by the differences between what I had learned about shooting at Wentworth and the differences in style and substance in the Marine Corps. Old Sergeant Blue used to throw his sling over his arm when he shot, but the system in the Corps was much different. We used the sling in shooting in a way that I had never seen before, and when I finally mastered the method I had no trouble in holding the gun just where I wanted it. One afternoon we went out and fired with a telescope sight at 800 yards. I had never seen one used before. It was quite a bit like sighting through a surveying instrument. There were two cross hairs in the telescope which was attached to the sighting apparatus, and by placing their intersection on the bulls-eye and gently squeezing the trigger, it was pretty easy to make a good score. An old Swede sergeant, who was an expert shot, adjusted the sights and then turned the rifles over to us. At 800 yards I had no trouble in putting the shots all in the bulls-eye.

In our last week at Winthrop, we shot the preliminary to our Army record course, and because of the fact that I had been working hard at the shooting game and learning my gun and the sighting fine points, I came through with 266—13 points more than is needed for "expert rifleman." I figured that it would be the best thing for me to make good at whatever they put us at; so while a good many of the boys loafed on the job, I worked with the various positions as much as I could. One other fellow ran me a close race in the preliminaries, in fact we were tied up to the last range, where I beat him out by two points. Although I fell down to 262 on the afternoon we shot the record, I made the expert with 9 points to spare and shot more consistently than I had the day before. My lowest score at any range was 41 out of 50 and my highest was 46. I was disappointed though, because one man beat me out by two points. It was in the record shooting that our attention or inattention to details showed up. Three fellows who were excellent shots fell down on the last range because they didn't know their points of aim. We shot three strings of ten shots rapid fire in the course, and used what was known as battle sight, that is, we didn't change the elevation of the sights although we shot from 200, 300 and 500 yards. So it was necessary to aim sometimes at the very bottom of the target in order to hit the bulls-eye. We had been coached well to look out for this, but as I said some of the fellows came up to the last range with fine records, and then fell down miserably. There were only 5 out of the 116 young officers who made expert, and I am glad to say that both Ashurst and I were among the five. Wallace shot 256.

On the day I shot for the record, the enlisted man who was scoring for me asked me if I was any kin to Ovid Sellers—he was Nathan McClure, son of the President of McCormick Seminary, where my brother had earned his divinity degree and later would serve as Dean. McClure was a fine fellow, although he was a Yale student, and he told me a few stories of my oldest brother.

Many famous athletes from all across the country were in our group. We almost had an All-American football team in addition to the standout athletes from other sports. Quite a group came from Minnesota, including All-American Benny Bierman, later head football coach at Minnesota, and Bert Baston, the best end I have ever seen. He was on the team that beat us at the University of Chicago 49 to 0. Hal Jeschke, a fellow Chicago man, was the Big Ten champion wrestler at 135 pounds. Baston was a very funny man, and he used to wrestle with Jeschke in the quarters all the time. Bill Legore and Johnny Overton (who had horrible table manners) of Yale were both famous athletes as was Princeton's Bill Eddy. I also met a fellow from Tarkio, Missouri who had just graduated from Annapolis. It rather surprised me to learn that six midshipmen from Annapolis had joined the Marine Corps. I hadn't known that they ever came directly from the Academy into the Marine service.

While at Winthrop, I also had to attend to a few personal matters. In mid-July, I received Marine uniforms from the Marshall Field department store in Chicago. I had canceled my order with them by letter but they seemed to have had the crust to have sent them anyway. The breeches fit all right but the blouse fit in no way whatsoever. I didn't know what I could do with the thing, but I needed a uniform badly so I had it altered.

I owed my parents some money, about $200.00 dollars, which they hadn't been pressing me for but which debt I was anxious to eliminate as soon as possible. My pay for the last week in June, plus my traveling expenses was covered and I had $37.50 left. I had already advanced a large amount to cover my uniforms ordered in Washington, and I had paid what I owed the Quartermaster. So, with a certain level of responsibility I sent my parents a sum and promised to make regular payments after that. There was little for us to spend money on there unless we went into Washington on the weekends, so I was able to save my pennies.

My friend 2nd Lt Mordecai Chambers, USMCR, arrived on July 12, 1917 and I was soon aware of everything worth knowing about home. A few days before, 2nd Lt William W. Ashurst, USMC, and eleven other fellows were ordered to Quantico and we soon learned from them that they would go with their companies to Philadelphia on the 17th and then to France about the 19th. The rest of us had not been assigned to our charges though, and we didn't know when we would get action. The colonel told us that we would go to Quantico on the 20th to be assigned to our commands, but I never believed anything until I had received my orders.

3

QUANTICO

On Wednesday, July 18, we moved to the newly purchased Quantico facility in Virginia, where the 5th and 6th Marine Regiments were assembled and trained. The Marine Corps had only recently acquired Quantico at the time, and we were the first outfit trained at the base. Officers' Training Camp lasted three months, and while we were there, the Corps brought in enlisted recruits to fill the ranks of the 6th Regiment. These enlistees had been through boot camp at San Diego or Paris Island and were quite familiar with military discipline by the time they arrived at Quantico. The 5th Regiment was uniquely a composite unit for regulars from all over the world, and it had received its full complement of men first. The 6th Regiment needed lieutenants, and we were competing for the open officer positions.

Quantico looked just like pictures of mining towns I had seen. There was one small street which constituted the original town. This street led right up from the pier. Quantico was just four or five miles down the Potomac from Winthrop. Then there were rows and rows of unpainted wooden shacks, sprung up almost literally overnight. The small streets between were all cut up with rain wash, and we stumbled over what was left of a former small forest, roots and stumps, and sewer excavations. South of the town was another city of tents. The sounds of dogs and cats was always prevalent around Marine Camps, and they seemed to be always contented. Down town there were little restaurants where we could get an egg sandwich for 50 cents. And there was also a dance hall where they charged 20 cents for a dance with one of the painted ladies brought to town for the purpose. Between nearly every two tents, there were dummies for bayonet practice, and at all hours of the day enlisted men could be seen slaughtering these dummy Germans.

I learned from 2ndLt. William Wallace Ashurst, USMC, shortly after our arrival, that I almost got to join the company he was in. Seventeen men were selected from the gang at Winthrop to join the base detachment of the 5th Marine Regiment. Part of the 5th was already in Europe, and the battalion still at Quantico was going to join them in a short while to act as a reserve. The seventeen names were sent into headquarters and there they decided that only twelve men were needed. So the last five on the alphabetical list were cut out, and I was on that list. The following week, a lieutenant in Ashurst's company, 2ndLt. John H. McCahey, USMC, killed himself on July 16, 1917. When Captain Lester S. Wass, USMC, skipper of the 18th Company, 5th Marine Regiment, asked Wallace to recommend someone to take the place of the deceased, I was named, and the captain tried to get me designated, but headquarters, because of some red tape, wouldn't do it. So I lost out twice.

Our bunch from Winthrop was only part of the stream of young reserve officers which was pouring into the place. A detachment from Port Royal came the day after we did, another came from Paris Island, another from Chicago, and yet another from Mare Island. The train on which the Californians traveled was wrecked in Louisiana and two men were killed with 9 more hurt.

We had been divided into companies A, B, and C and would receive our training as units. A captain had charge of each company, and the impression we made on him was what would count in our records. I was surprised at what close record was kept of Marine officers. Whenever we changed our post or our commander was changed, in to headquarters went our fitness reports, in which our immediate commander was required to answer the most personal questions concerning us: our ability and efficiency. By the rounding up of those adversely reported on, the personnel of the officers in the Marine Corps was kept very high.

It amazed me how high the morale was in the Marine enlisted men also. Most of them were afraid of nothing and firmly believed that the Marine Corps would lead the allied armies through the streets of Berlin within a few months. I can still see those sturdy boys with 35-pound packs on their back, double-timing up and down the parade ground. Their commander was old Colonel Hiram I. Bearss, USMC, known as "Hiking Hiram." He was the most profane old slave driver you ever saw, and whenever he saw the companies move, he'd tell them to run. His battalion had been digging trenches for the previous two weeks, and Ashurst told me how he stormed at the officers because the dirt wasn't flying fast enough. The next day the officers told the men to throw the dirt just as high as they could when the Colonel came around. Wallace said that when old Hiram visited then, the trench looked like an artesian well.

Our program at Quantico was as follows: Reveille 5:45, Physical drill 6:00, Breakfast 6:30, Drill 7:30 - 9:30, Inspection of quarters 11:45, Dinner 12:00, Drill 1:00 - 2:30, 3:00 - 4:00, Supper 6:00, Study 7:00 - 9:00, Taps 10:00. The physical drill before breakfast consisted of running about a half mile in the company streets. As I have described about the condition of the streets, these runs were a regular obstacle course. Captain Philip H. Torrey, USMC, of Company "A" told his men that in order to stay in the Marine Corps they had to have "guts and efficiency, and especially the former." One of our boys keeled over after the first run, and another had to be taken to a hospital in Washington with appendicitis.

Our Captain, George H. Barrett, USMC, in "C" Company, seemed to be a perfect gentleman and treated us as such. He was a very good drillmaster, and I liked to work under him. For the first three days we drilled without guns, executing the first movements of the school of the squad and company only. Then we started out with the semaphore code, for which I made up some cards with the code written on one side of the card and the meaning written on the other, in accordance with my brother Ovid's system, and soon fairly well mastered the alphabet.

We quickly settled down into a regular routine, and a hard tiresome one it was in that climate. Rains occurred nearly every night, and the sun shone all day, making a sultry oppressive heat that was almost unbearable to the boys from the north. Heat had never bothered me much and I didn't feel many ill effects, thank goodness. Our commanders, with an eye on the weather, did not work us as hard as they might, and we gradually became fit. We had not yet received guns and so we drilled without arms. But even thus, when we returned from drill our clothes were wringing wet.

My military training at Wentworth stood me in good stead at Quantico, as the shooting did at Winthrop; so I had the jump on most of the fellows, even those who had come from places like Virginia Military Institute and Culver Military Academy. Our captain placed particular stress upon attention to details in the manner of giving and executing commands, and I had no reason to think that he had been less than pleased with my work. Out of the more than 240 officer trainees, 12 were selected to go on duty as Officers of the Day, and I was fortunate enough to be among them, even though my duties interrupted my plans to go to Washington D.C. on the weekend.

The base battalion of the 5th Marine Regiment, to which Ashurst had been assigned, had been delayed on account of lack of equipment. So every day we saw them drilling on the parade ground and making practice marches along the roads. They had to carry their packs on their backs during all drills, even the officers were thus encumbered, and they doubled time a great deal with their 9 pound rifles and their 35 pound packs jingling along.

On Thursday, July 26, the Major General Commandant, George Barnett, USMC, came down to look the battalion over, and the bunch looked as fit as a fiddle. There was very little of pomp and display; and even when the Commandant was there, we had no blaring of brass bands, no dressing up of the troops. The inspection was not to ascertain whether the men could conduct a beautiful parade; it was to find out whether they were ready to go.

More officers were coming in all the time. A batch came in from the east—big strapping foot-ball players from Harvard, Princeton and Yale. There were by then four companies in the Officers Training School with about eighty men to a company. Captains from the regulars were in charge of us, and we were put through the paces. Over at Winthrop the informality was noticeable; there was no saluting, except when the colonel was near, and there were no restrictions or prescribed rules as to dress. At Quantico though, structured discipline prevailed and woe be to the man late to formations or slack in his duties. Our Captain Barrett treated us as brother officers so long as we watched our step; but he was capable of giving unmerciful bawlings out as several of the fellows could bear witness.

About twelve lieutenants came in from Winthrop, who had risen from the ranks. One of them, 2ndLt Lothar R. Long,

USMC, I discovered was a brother of my old Beta Theta Pi fraternity mates, Ed and Al Long. He himself was a Beta from Northwestern. He had been a reporter in Seattle, and growing tired of the work, had enlisted in the Marine Corps and shipped for China. He came back in 1917 and passed the examination for a second lieutenancy. He told me he knew my brother Sandy at Chicago. Two more Betas came from Wisconsin also, but there was not much opportunity for fraternizing.

Mordecai and I purchased a washboard, a big brush, and a few bars of Fils-Naptha soap. I did my week's wash in one afternoon, an unusual occupation for me. If we didn't do our own washing, we would be in a bad way for clothes, because we had to change at least twice during the day because we sweated so much. I usually went right into the shower with my underclothes on and sometimes my trousers and shirt also.

By the second week of August, 1917, there had been practically no change in our routine, except that a cool wave enlivened everyone. Our drills ran much more smoothly, and the boys felt twice as well as before. During our rest periods we had been picking up the semaphore code which added somewhat to the variety. Our company had been divided for the last two weeks into ten permanent squads, and I was fortunate enough to be chosen as a squad leader. We had no other organization. The man whose commission dated earliest was our first sergeant, but there were no lieutenants or sergeants; at each drill one complete squad was dissected, and its members provided the officers for the company.

Captain Barrett watched us very carefully and graded us after each trial; everything was done to show us that we were to be selected according to our zeal and ability, but we didn't know for what we would be picked. There were all sorts of rumors, some of them partly substantiated, others entirely groundless. The best founded one was that about 40 of our school would be sent with the 6th Marine Regiment, our next overseas detachment. Our captain virtually told us that such was the case, but he also remarked that none of us yet had sufficient experience to start right out in charge of a platoon. In a personal talk I had with him, he said that several of the boys who went with the 5th Marine Regiment were shoved in prematurely, and were acquiring bad efficiency records already.

I received three shots for typhoid and the first two really affected me; the third didn't put me as far under the weather. I tried going to Washington right after my second shot and felt dopey all the time I was there. The following Saturday night one of the boys took me to a private dance at the home of Washington's Unitarian preacher. I livened up a bit that evening, but I slept all the next day, so by Monday I was all right again.

One day while we were drilling, a strange captain came up and gave us the once over. We thought that he was a regular officer, and we were strutting around in great shape to show off before him. Presently, after a little conference with Capt. George H. Barrett, USMC, he took charge of us and started in giving commands. He tied us all up, and we began thinking something was wrong when he commanded "Column Right About," there being no such command. All of us were doing our best to keep serious, but there were many stifled outbursts of laughter. We found out later that our unknown commander was Capt. Drexel A. J. Biddle, USMCR, prominent Philadelphia millionaire and athlete. He enlisted, by his own methods, 2000 Marines, and seemed to be commendably interested in the organization. He was given a commission as a reserve captain, a kind of honorary office, but he had been assigned to this post and was trying to learn his duties as best he could. Although a grandfather, he was still a very active boxer and polo player, so Captain Barrett informed us.

Practically all we did at Quantico was drill and dig trenches. We did not have any real combat training, map reading, or other obligatory requirements for survival in the field. And our trenches were anything but standard. We just dug wherever we were and whatever the contour of the ground would call for. They varied a great deal in size and depth but were usually over 5 or 6 feet deep. In drill, my Wentworth training was valuable, even though the close and extended order drill that I was taught at the Academy was completely changed on at least three separate occasions during our training.

My friend 2nd Lt. Mordecai Chambers, USMC, did not seem to be making a great deal of an impression on the captain. He was too good-natured, slow, and easygoing to make progress along military lines, and I rather feared for him. The two of us went to Washington D.C. for a weekend in the middle of August. While there, I purchased shoes, boots, and a few other trifles, not enough to occupy me for more than an hour. Remembering that my mother told me that Ben Hoge, a Wentworth classmate, had been stationed at Ft. Myer, Mordecai and I called on him, and we were soon invited out to have lunch with Ben and his wife. His wife was a charming girl and she appeared to be just as genuine as Ben. They had not been able to get permanent quarters and were considering moving into Washington. But while we were lunching at the officer's club, they received news that quarters right at the fort had been procured for them, and they were much elated. After inviting them in to supper with us, Mordecai and I went out to see a ball game between Washington and the Chicago White Sox, a team that included the infamous "Shoeless" Joe Jackson. The game was well worth seeing, and we got back in plenty of time to meet Ben and his wife. We had a good supper and went to the theatre afterwards. The following morning, Sunday, I was under the weather again. A good many of the boys were having trouble with their stomachs, and I came in for my share that Sunday morning. I slept all day and went to see the doctor when I got back to Quantico that night. He fixed me up with the old standby dose of castor oil, and I almost immediately came around.

On August 13, the entire Officers' Training Camp was put

into a little group all its own. We spent the entire day chopping out stumps, raking up wood chips, and cleaning house generally. We were then more comfortably located than formerly. We actually got a little breeze occasionally and we had more room all around. In our shack we had five tables in one end for writing and studying.

On August 14, I learned that I had been designated to go to the 6th Marine Regiment which was then forming at Quantico in preparation to go to France as the next Marine overseas force. Our captain called his squad leaders into his office and told us that he was going to give us the best details he could get for us because we had worked well for him. Then we heard through round about channels that when he was ordered to designate men for the Sixth, he sent in the names of second rate men in the company. Headquarters fired them back to him and said he must send his best men. So he called in the selected men and gave us the good news. They picked many of us who had come from military schools as well as a few well-drilled college graduates to become platoon leaders, and thus the 6th Regiment was born.

We expected to join our companies within a week, but none of us knew what he would get. I initially believed that I might draw a machine gun assignment, but I didn't know whether I would accept that branch or not. Everybody was crazy to go, and we who were drawn were objects of envy to the rest of the boys. I was not particularly anxious to join in the European festivities, but somehow in spite of my better judgment, I was glad and willing to go. Another thing that pleased me was that those of us who would go now, unlike Ashurst's bunch, had been selected purely on merit and not on snap judgments of men who hardly knew us by name. We knew that we probably would not leave Quantico before the first of October, because it took time to mobilize a whole Marine regiment, about 2,700 men, and we should have a hard row to hoe whipping our men into shape. The organization of the Marine companies was being modeled after the U.S. Army, TO&E of 1917, and they were huge affairs of about 250 men. I would be in command of a platoon and have to be responsible to a great extent for their efficiency. So I had bitten off a pretty big chunk when my experience was considered. But I felt that I could handle the job as well as the next one.

In late August, I reported to the 2nd Battalion and was assigned to my platoon, the first of the 78th Company. The 2nd Battalion was composed of the 78th (E), the 79th (F), the 80th (G), and the 96th (H) Companies. The Battalion Commander was Major Thomas Holcomb, USMC, later Commandant of the Marine Corps at the outbreak of the Second World War. About 250 men were assigned to each company. The 6th Regiment consisted of three battalions along with the 73rd Machine Gun Company.

The 5th and 6th Marine Regiments, along with the 6th Machine Gun Battalion (USMC), were the only Marine units to see combat in France. These Marines formed the 4th Brigade (Marine) serving in the 2nd United States Army Infantry Division. Besides these Marine regiments, the 2nd Division, AEF, was composed of the 9th and 23rd U.S. Infantry Regiments, the 12th, 15th, and 17th U.S. Field Artillery Regiments, the 2nd Engineer Regiment, the 4th, 5th, and 6th Machine Gun Battalions (USMC), and the various headquarters and peripheral units necessary to every division. In all, the Division was comprised of 28,000 men.

Our unit was led by some first rate officers. The company commander of the 96th Company was Capt. Donald F. Duncan, USMC, a scion of a very old family from St. Joseph, Missouri and a graduate of Culver Military Academy in Indiana. Captain Duncan would later be killed in action at Bouresches, France during the Battle of Belleau Wood. He was in his early thirties as were most of the company commanders, but they seemed so old to us who were so young. I had just celebrated my twenty-second birthday as I arrived at Winthrop.

25

The four company commanders in the battalion were all men who had been commissioned for 13 or 14 years. Though our cadres were mostly composed of very green officers, the four company commanders all had considerable experience. The 78th Company Commander was Capt. Robert E. Messersmith, USMC. Five lieutenants, including me, were under his command. The other four were 2ndLt. James P. Adams, USMC, from Clemson University; 2ndLt. Paul S. Taylor, USMC, from the University of Wisconsin, not much of a physical specimen; 1stLt. Julius C. Coggswell, USMC, from South Carolina University who would later be badly wounded in action during the Battle of Belleau Wood; and 1stLt. Amos R. Shinkle, USMC, an old farmer-like sort of fellow who had not attended college.

On my first day as a platoon leader, I reported to the captain for duty, and he told me to get settled that afternoon and go to drill the next morning. Our company was infantry, but the first morning of drill our Major put me in charge of a newly formed Machine gun platoon, composed of one squad from each company in the battalion. Since there were three battalions, there were three platoons, and three green lieutenants in charge of them. We drew our guns the next morning and then received instruction in the mechanism and drill. From our orders we had no idea of what part we should take in the regiment, because there was a machine gun battalion, a separate organization from the infantry. So we blindly obeyed orders.

The man who instructed us was an old time Marine. He had seen something like 20 years active service as an enlisted man, and he took great pride in his commission, which he had recently received. He reminded me somewhat of Sergeant Blue at Wentworth; he had the same set military phraseology, and the same fondness for using big words wrongly. The first afternoon we were out, he instructed us in the nomenclature of the gun. He would name off the parts of the different plates and then would ask some man to do the same. One youngster was doing this in a frightened haphazard sort of way, and 2ndLt.

Thomas J. Curtis, USMC, yelled out, "Name those parts proper and chronological, and don't be ambiguous." This order seemed to impress the men very much; so they strove all the harder. His entire audience of Marine officers were recent college graduates, but not a one of us even cracked a smile at his fractured grammar.

We were issued one Lewis machine gun to a squad and I was lucky in having a corporal who was a graduate of the Lewis gun school in Utica, New York, and he was of considerable aid to me during the instruction periods. The men in my platoon were all young eager boys who were willing to work their fingers off for us. By little ways I let my men know that I wanted our platoon to show up the other platoons, and in the squad, whichever man proved to be the most adept at dismounting and assembling the gun, I put into the coveted position of Number One, the firer. I found that in this way no bullying or cursing out was necessary to keep them going.

We worked at the mechanism and nomenclature all week, varying it with a simulated selection of gun emplacements against fancied Germans. All my men were very much absorbed in the game of creeping up behind cover, placing the gun and directing their aim. All this work was on top of a wooded hill behind our camp, where there was plenty of shade and quiet, and I enjoyed every minute of the work tremendously.

But on August 26, the three of us who were in charge of the platoons were summoned to the office of Major Edward B. Cole, USMC, the 6th Marine Regimental Machine Gun officer. He informed us that we were to get no more instruction, but that we should assume the role of instructors from then on. Every infantry company in the regiment drew 8 guns two days later, and our platoon resumed their role within the company as an infantry platoon but with machine guns. It fell upon my shoulders to instruct three green platoons and their officers in the intricacies of the Lewis gun. Of course my platoon had to assist, but the burden of the job rested on my shoulders. I found it hard to imagine that I, who hadn't seen a Lewis gun but a few days before and who previously had an aversion to machinery, was now in the position of being the resident expert.

I studied like a fiend on the operation of the gun with the result that the evening of the third day of instruction I took the gun apart and put it together blindfolded. It was very important that all the men were taught to do this, because so much machine gun work was done in the dark. I never before liked to tinker with a hammer, but I certainly fell into machine gun work. I counted myself fortunate to have had the opportunity of doing that work, but I still haven't the least idea as to how the major happened to strike on me to do it.

However, the Lewis guns were soon taken away and placed on airplanes, so I returned to my regular platoon assignment. We continued our training, including physical training, bayonet practice, marches, and bivouacs. We also switched to mock trench fighting instead of digging. Discipline among the men was excellent throughout this. We had no trouble at all. These men had been through boot camp and were in good shape physically and mentally. As for weapons, the men were issued only the 1903 Springfield rifles, while the officers were given Colt .45 caliber automatic pistols along with the Springfields.

During these months our company adopted a mascot, a bulldog named Dixie, which had been given to our first sergeant by his girlfriend. We did not have any trouble with him at Quantico. I would write letters home with him in my lap, and he would insist that I hold him a certain way until he dozed off, wheezing and snoring like a fat traveling man. He was as fat as a pig and spoiled to death, but he was the cutest little animal that I had ever seen. When we were getting ready to board ship in Philadelphia, Dixie tangled with a visiting dog. Dixie had bulldog instinct but no fighting experience. He survived this little fracas however, and accompanied us overseas. We trained him before we went up to the lines so he would stay with us. Dixie was very much a member of the company and a great boost for morale.

Major Holcomb was far-sighted, and gradually we were getting our equipment in shape under his direction at the same time we were drilling and Captain Messersmith was a great hand to get ahead of others when it came to equipment; so we were very nearly ready to shove off at any time. A queer situation had arisen in our company in the matter of rank of the officers, which gave the captain some trouble. 1stLt. Shinkle, who had been acting as the senior and assistant to the captain, was found to be the second ranking lieutenant, and the boy Coggswell, who was senior, was the most inexperienced one of us all. He was a good lad, but rather irresponsible and forgetful of his dignity as an officer. Besides he had a high squeaky voice which was the bane of the captain's existence. It didn't affect me in the least, because I was the third ranking lieutenant, and although that was the case, the captain let me keep the first platoon.

On September 28, we got in a new bunch of twenty recruits from Port Royal. They had received very little instruction in drill, and the captain turned them over to me for instruction. They were quite different from the other men in the company in that they were dopey slow and indifferent. I took them one morning, and as soon as I found out their spirit, I put them through the paces quite differently from my usual custom. The captain told me to give them a good work out, and I certainly did. Ordinarily with my own platoon, I would give them a good snappy drill, which they performed eagerly and in fine fettle, and then let them rest. But these men needed to be driven; so although I hated to do it, I worked them until their tongues hung out and they couldn't go any farther. I didn't think that when they would be scattered into the various platoons that many of them would land in mine, because they were rather small, and I had the larger fellows in my first platoon.

At about this time, several of the officers in the battalion had received letters from Marine officers overseas in which they complained that the 5th Regiment had been split up. Various companies had been assigned to guard duty—longshoremen's tasks—with one company, the 67th Co. (D), going to England for routing duty. I thought at the time that if that was the case, we should have good billets when we did get across. In fact I wouldn't have been surprised if that rumor were true, because patrolling had always been the strong point of the Marines. I did not think it would have been all that bad to conduct a provost guard in some French city. But we knew that there was no use in counting upon such a thing of that kind, because there were so many rumors afloat that not much stock could be placed in any of them.

I also no longer had to do my own washing. I had an orderly, a small Jewish man named Glucksman, who was a peach. He could hardly speak English, but he could certainly wash clothes. I had a hard time keeping him from washing my stuff before it got dirty. When I returned from home I had three shirts, besides the one on my back. I had worn only one of them for one day, but when I came back from the first day's drill, I couldn't find any of them. I found out that Glucksman had taken everything he could find and was washing it. Whenever I told him he had made a good job of washing something he felt as pleased as he could be, and it hurt his feelings tremendously when I didn't let him know at once when I had more for him to do.

I began giving the boys some new wrinkles in bayonet fighting. I didn't know much about it myself, but by experimenting a little, I found a new stroke or two that could be used in fencing; so I had half of my men get long stakes, and let the other men use their bayonets and made them go to it in good shape. They parried and thrusted with a little too much energy though, and in spite of my precautions, they occasionally became somewhat too eager, and a few of them received slight cuts on the hands. Shortly after inaugurating the new system a good many of the other lieutenants who noticed it came around for a little of the dope. I found that I could always get better results out of the boys if I inserted a little of the spirit of competition into the exercises.

So, I kept before them constantly the idea that they wanted to be the best-drilled organization around. We were supposed to have weekly competitive drills between the platoons of the company, but we had them only twice and my platoon won both of them. So I felt satisfied.

Sometimes we were summoned for less mundane duties. Once, the 78th Company was chosen to act for the movies. The play in which we appeared was a seven reel feature entitled "The Three Things," and although we did not have a large hand in the production, we staged a very pretty attack from our trenches, which should have looked well in the movies. That was one of the first times in which we sported our helmets, the real American official trench headdress. They were made of steel and painted a dark greenish brown color. Inside they were fitted with a sort of net which fits the head, and between the net and steel casing, there were little rubber tube sections which were so placed as to take the shock of a blow. They were comfortable enough, but nevertheless they grew mighty heavy before the day was over.

The hot 1917 summer dragged on into fall. In early October the weather turned cold and consequently, nearly all our time was taken up in trying to keep warm. However, we succeeded in stealing a stove for our company office, so from then on, I was able to process paperwork and write there in comfort. To add to our troubles we had gotten in a number of new recruits for the company, and it was necessary to work nights, getting them equipped for cold weather. In the latter part of October we had been working nights and when not working we gathered around the office stove for warmth. It was the only place where we could get warm.

Our time of departure had again been postponed, and none

of us knew when we'd get away. I really didn't believe we would pull out before the first of November, although most estimates put the date before that. I wasn't correct since it was to be much later than my guess but I was closer than most of the other fellows.

I went into Washington D.C. again the second weekend of October. I caught a show in the afternoon, and in the evening I visited Ben Hoge at Ft. Myer. Ben's company was giving a dance so I interloped, and had a very good time. The next afternoon I took a wild shot and called up Virginia Eckels, the very pretty little sister of one of my fraternity brothers whose family lived just half a block from our fraternity house in Chicago. I visited her at Miss Maderra's School. I visited her that afternoon; it was quite an experience with all those girls peeking at me from their windows.

On October 18, I received notice from the Department of the Navy that I had temporarily been appointed a first lieutenant. This included no change in my assignment or duties, but I appreciated the pay raise of $25.00 per month; so I was then drawing about $182.00 per month, not bad at all for me. We still received very little training in such things as Signal Corps operations, radio, and communications. Instead the propensity for trench digging, bayonet training, and range fire seemed never-ending.

Few recreational facilities were available at Quantico. The Y.M.C.A. did sponsor band concerts. We also had boxing and wrestling one night a week and motion pictures every night but Sunday. Also, a troop of vaudevillians came down from Washington D.C. every week. On weekends we had free time, and most of us went to Washington. I wore my dress blues to Washington on one occasion and went to Keith's Theatre. A woman approached me and asked me to show her to her seat. Many people at that time did not recognize a Marine uniform. She thought me an usher.

Washington was a rather sleepy town then, and I soon

found more pleasant diversions. I had a large, good-natured Marine friend named 2ndLt. George G. "Fuzzy" Munce, USMC, a V.M.I. graduate from Richmond, Virginia. I made a few trips there with him during the fall and was in excellent hands. It was very much like getting back home. "Fuzzy" was one of my fellow lieutenants at Quantico but in the 6th Regimental machine gun company (73rd). He had invited me down to visit him; I accepted the invitation and had such a fine time, and got such a cordial welcome that I went back again. Mr. John Munce, his father, was superintendent of the Kingan Packing Company; a very well-to-do man, hailing from Ireland. The entire family, except a maiden aunt, were very robust, averaging about 200 pounds per capita, and their hearts were as big as their bodies, proportionately.

There were three boys and the father, Mrs. Munce having died sometime before. Miss Hester Gilliam, her sister, was the housekeeper. She was very thin, and I had the secret conviction that she was so thin because of her efforts to rustle provisions for the family. I received this impression after the first meal I had with them. I had developed an enormous appetite at Quantico, but I got more than I could handle at the Munce table. I was compelled, almost literally, to eat two pieces of steak, two pieces of chicken and innumerable vegetables at that first meal. We ended up with peach shortcake as a dessert, and I could barely negotiate it. As soon as I thought my duty was performed, in came a quarter section of thick pumpkin pie from the next door neighbor, who had heard that I was from Missouri. I grinned sickly, and the good people thought I was champing the bit to get at the pie. I certainly deserve credit for my attack on that pie, and I am proud to say that I conquered it. After my exhibition at the table I was readily admitted into the family circle as one worthy of the best. Fuzzy kept care of me in the social line just as well as in the gastronomic. I had as a partner to a dance at the country club, the daughter of the mayor of Richmond, and a very good looker she was too. I dated another charming girl there as well, but I did not get very far; she was a Catholic.

On Sunday, we all went to the Presbyterian Church and I was introduced into a Sunday School class, and there too was given a warm reception. The Munce Family were very zealous church workers. Mr. Munce was Superintendent of the Sunday School and an Elder. A Dr. Cecil was pastor of the church I attended and had been so for the past seventeen years. Before him old Dr. Hoge reigned for something like fifty years, I was told. I wondered if he was not some kin to our Hoges. It seemed to me that I had heard Colonel Hoge, Wentworth's principal and the father of Ben and Bill, speak of him, and I remembered that most of his ancestors and kinfolk were preachers. In the afternoon I was given an automobile ride over the city and was shown all the historic points of interest, and there seemed to be a million of them. We had a few of the fair sex along with us on the trip to lend interest.

In the evening, just before we left for Quantico, we had evening family prayers, which I found out was the regular program for every evening when the family was there in full force. After my first visit with them I went back three times, twice after Fuzzy had left for Europe. The Munce's certainly added to my pleasures while I was at Quantico, and the weekend excursions were a welcome break from our training. The more I saw of them, the less I wondered about the love of Virginians for their state. They were absolutely the most hospitable and elegant people I ever met, and I met many of their friends who were like them. After church services during my last visit in November, I received about four invitations to dinner from people who were strangers to me. Everyone down there was trying to do something for the soldiers, and a uniform was your passport wherever you went. At that last Sunday dinner with the Munces, I met a Dr. Lingle, who said that he had preached the baccalaureate sermon for Wentworth three years before and that he remembered my parents well. He was a professor at a theological seminary in Richmond and was President of the board at Davidson College.

It was about this time that I decided to take out $10,000.00 insurance with the Government, payable to my folks. It was straight life insurance and very cheap, in fact so cheap that nearly the entire enlisted personnel of the battalion took out the same amount. As Major Holcomb said, our battalion would be insured with the Government for about $10,000,000.00 and for fear of losing such an amount, we could be sure that we would be safely convoyed to Europe.

But in late October, we were still as much at sea about when our departure would be. The First Battalion, along with 6th Marine Regimental Headquarters Company, Supply Company, the Regimental Machine Gun Company (73rd), the Regimental Band, and the 6th Marine Regimental Commanding Officer Colonel Albertus W. Catlin, USMC, and his staff had all departed Quantico for Europe. It didn't stand to reason that they would keep us there much longer. The work was really becoming monotonous and we had advanced as far as we could in this country. It taxed our ingenuity to keep the men interested. We had all our equipment except for a few articles of winter field clothing, and were rapidly closing the gap on that. The 8th Regiment of Marines was now mobilizing at Quantico for tropical duty, and to remain much longer would cramp us for space. Needless to say, we were getting more and more anxious every day to shove off from Quantico. It appeared that the 3rd Battalion was going to leave before the 2nd, although there was nothing certain about that since their orders were changed twice on one day. It seemed that the army was holding us up by not being ready to embark when they said they would, and we had to wait for them in order to fill up the convoys.

My regular work with my platoon was still eminently satisfactory, although as I said it was becoming somewhat monotonous. During this time a rather amusing occurrence took place which affected my platoon. We were sitting up in the office at about ten minutes of ten, when a guard came up to the door with two of my men as prisoners. The men had just been arrested and I was rather curious to know what had been their offense. They were two very conscientious, hardworking, quiet boys, and I was very much surprised to see them under guard. It seems that they had been taken in connection with the theft of some ice cream from a druggist here. They were very sheepish and forlorn when they were brought up to get their blankets, which they had to do in order to spend the night in the "brig." It seems that four other Marines had stolen the ice cream, and these two men had been invited to partake. When they were searching for the booty, which had been hidden, they were caught by the patrol. The evidence looked rather bad for them.

The next morning, they were taken up before the major for office hours, at which time offenders are arraigned, and if their offense is worthy of a trial, the time for the trial is set. I went down to be present and see if I could do anything for them. After the evidence was given, I got an opportunity to tell the major that the men were good, reliable fellows from my platoon, and to plead for clemency. The major gave me no satisfaction however, and I rather feared that the boys might get into some serious trouble over the affair. That night I heard that they were to be given a Summary Court Martial, and I persuaded the captain to go down next morning and plead for them. However, next morning before office hours, at drill, the major called me over and asked me if I still thought the men deserving of clemency. When I told him that I did, he said that he thought they were sufficiently scared to have learned a good lesson, and that he was going to let them off with paying the price of the cream. I was indeed pleased. The major evidently told the men when he let them off that I had spoken a good word for them, and they came up to me rather pathetically to thank me for my assistance in getting them out.

By showing the men in small ways that I was interested in

them, I was getting results that pleased me considerably. I had, for instance, gotten them outfitted with clothing sooner, or rather more completely, than any other platoon commander; every one of my men had an overcoat, yet in the company there were 62 overcoats shy right then. I was far from an experienced platoon leader yet, but I was rather proud of the way I got the men under me to work for me. The captain, and even the major, had a time or two remarked very favorably on my platoon, and it made me feel pretty good. I found that it was very seldom necessary or advisable to bawl my men out, and they stepped just as lively, in fact a little more so for me than any other bunch I saw around there.

I might give a little character sketch of each of the officers of my company. Captain Messersmith was of Dutch descent and came from Pennsylvania Dutch stock; when he was feeling good he gave us imitations of the way the old folks down there talk. He was a man of rather strong likes and dislikes, and strange to say, he was very much down on the Y.M.C.A. He believed that most of the young men who went into that work were doing so because they didn't want to fight, and he also didn't like them because he said they didn't help the chaplains out the way they should. So although the Y.M.C.A. had splendid performances there every week and moving pictures every night except Sunday, he would not attend any of them.

1stLt. Amos R. Shinkle, USMC, was an old hand at soldiering, having been an enlisted man for four years. He was very capable, illiterate, and amusing. The captain overrode the usual custom of putting the most senior ranking man as the Executive Officer of the company, and Shinkle acted in that capacity. He was absolutely unlearned in books, having never graduated from grammar school, but in common sense he was there with the goods. As an example of his adaptability and intelligence, he prepared for his examination to enter the Marine Corps in six weeks without any outside help to speak of at all. He had never completed a good course in arithmetic, but he learned in that time enough about algebra, geometry and plane trigonometry to pass the examination, which I think was rather remarkable. It was really a shame that he never had a chance to go to school. He had been helping to support his family ever since he was thirteen, and he had had to do day laboring most of the time, although he became a rather skillful carpenter before he entered the Marine Corps as a private. At that time he was then about 26 years old and beyond reclamation in the matter of speech.

He told me one day that he had just received a letter from his mother saying, "Why haven't you wrote? We don't know where you're at." Shink told me that he would rather spend money to buy a picture than write a letter. He said that he would send a picture of the company home, then his mother would look at it, see it was marked from Quantico, and therefore know he was here. He was one who was worse than I about writing. His mind was like a single track railroad; there was no switching him off a subject until he had thoroughly exhausted his views upon it, and had explained down to the minutest details every item, no matter how simple. I suppose he got that habit from explaining things to enlisted men. As an enlisted man, he had served on the President's yacht. He did not like that assignment, and as he told it, he would put a request for transfer every morning on his commander's desk.

2ndLt. Julius C. Coggswell, USMC, was from Charleston, South Carolina and was the youngest lieutenant in the company, although the ranking one. He took his examination for entrance into the Corps back in April 1917, and for that reason was given higher rank than the rest of us. He was well meaning but very kiddish and irresponsible, and more or less of a joke in the company.

2ndLt. Paul S. Taylor, USMC, was a fine upright boy from Sioux City, Iowa, who graduated from Wisconsin in 1916. He was a Phi Beta Kappa brother of mine, although I did not find it out until late November. In addition, he was an accomplished debater, and he had started out on a course of law when the war broke out. He never had much military experience before he joined the Marine Corps, but he picked up enough in the Officers' Training School to be selected among the first for active duty. He was very intelligent, adaptable, tactful, gentlemanly, and conscientious.

2ndLt. James P. Adams, USMC, was another boy from the South, and he attended Clemson University. His home was in Augusta, Georgia. He was bright and a big goodhearted animal, but waded through things like a blunderbuss. He and I coached a company football team, and his contributions were less than helpful. The captain had been very opposed to having a team until the 79th Company had blossomed out with a team that has beaten everything at the Post. The 79th Co. was the next company to ours, and they were bragging about their team so much that the captain had consented to let us organize. We had hardly any equipment, in fact, none to practice with. So before our first game, which we had with the 79th Co. second team, we had only run signals two afternoons. We played them and came out 12 to 0. I thought that since we had won our first game, we should find it easier to get things going for the rest of our schedule. We also paired up against the 96th Company, before gunning for the first team of the 79th Co.

Some of the old-timers were fascinating to us, and a great deal of help to a young officer. I had a weather-beaten old noncom named (GySgt.) George N. Lyman for my gunnery sergeant who had served several enlistments. The gunnery sergeant really ran the platoon. When the platoon was given an assignment, the platoon leader delegated responsibilities, but the sergeant made certain the enlisted men carried out their duties. Despite our age difference and his far greater experience, Lyman always addressed me as "sir," and military courtesy was always maintained. But when he gave me advice, I listened carefully and was grateful for his assistance. Lyman took a fatherly interest in me, becoming a loyal friend. When we were about to sail, he gave me a bottle of

Eno's Fruit Salt, which he thought was good for seasickness. I appreciated his concern about his lieutenant's first ocean voyage. The sixty men in the platoon had a great deal of respect for him also. As the 1st Platoon was composed of the tallest men of the company, any one of them could physically have broken the diminutive GySgt. Lyman in two. Yet every afternoon when the GySgt. had his nap, you could hear a pin drop in the barracks.

The most famous of the Marine noncoms was 1stSgt. Daniel J. Daly in our regimental machine gun company. He was awarded two Medal of Honors during his illustrious career in China and Haiti, and he was widely known as one of the great old Marines. 1stSgt. Daly did not give the appearance of a hard-boiled Marine noncom; he was quite handsome and gave the appearance of being a perfect gentleman. Daly's unit was sometimes attached to ours; so it was quite natural for a number of us very green lieutenants to find where Daly's platoon was billeted and gather around Daly in the cool of the evenings after we had drilled all day. 1stSgt. Daly thoroughly enjoyed having an audience of gullible rookie lieutenants. He particularly enjoyed using nautical terms with which we had not been familiar before.

The battalion commander, Maj. Thomas Holcomb, USMC, and the adjutant, 2ndLt. Pere Wilmer, USMCR, were the only officers who were mounted. I don't know how he managed it, but 1stSgt. Daly was the only noncom I had ever heard of who had his own mount and an orderly, whom he called a "striker." On one occasion Daly complained about his orderly, reporting that "This darn striker was so ignorant that he tried to get me to mount the starboard gang of my horse instead of the port gang." Naturally we tried to steer our conversation so as to give Daly the opportunity of displaying his seagoing vocabulary. So on another occasion, we reported to him that we heard that a number of nurses and telephone operator girls would be on the ship when we would sail to Europe. To this scuttlebutt Daly said, "I don't want to be no shipmates with no women." This gave us the opportunity for someone to ask whether he had had some trouble with the ladies. "Yes," he said, "I saved up $800 and give it to her and she runs off with a coxswain of a trolley car!"

I do not remember any thievery within the unit, but much existed between branches, and 1stSgt. Daly was notorious in this field. When Daly went to the supply outfit, everybody showed up to see what he would get away with. A good thief who could steal from the Quartermaster or the food unit was highly regarded. Daly was so skillful at thievery that when he went to the Quartermaster for supplies, all hands would drop everything in an attempt to keep Daly from stealing them blind. I cannot vouch for the truth of this story, but it was reported that when we first landed in France at St. Nazaire, we boarded trains for a short trip inland to a training area. By the time we arrived, all the gasoline that was to be used for the Colonel's lamps was in Daly's possession. Dan was supposed to have been very embarrassed after he had learned of his mistake. As he went over the top at Belleau Woods, he shouted the famous rallying cry, 'Come on, you sons-of-bitches, do you want to live forever?"

Rumors were flying about our departure. One was that we would be sent to Mexico. Even the Captain fueled the rumor mill after returning from Washington D.C. in mid-November. He implied in a very mysterious way that he had the dope that we were going to shove off for France in a week and a half. I hoped that he was right, but I had become rather skeptical of all rumors by then. Soon thereafter, I read in the paper that General Pershing said that no Marines would go into the trenches before a brigade had been formed in France. That news was discouraging to me and to all the others. I, and everyone I had spoken with at Quantico, wanted to go to France. But our wanting didn't help us to get there. I also wished that I could have gotten home for my sister Pauline's wedding but that was another disappointment.

We had pretty good food while at Quantico, but our galleys were primitive. Our mess sergeant, Sgt. Lee S. Turner, was an old timer who had spent a number of years in the Marines. On Thanksgiving Day, most officers had gone on leave, and 1stLt. Amos Shinkle and I were the only ones left with the company. I had thought I would be going to Richmond, VA for the Thanksgiving holiday to visit with the Munce family. But after learning that their son Marshall, a contemporary of mine who took charge of me when I visited Richmond, was going on a visit at that time, I thought it best not to accept the invitation of that most hospitable family. So I stayed at Quantico Thursday and Friday in the company of 1stLt. Shinkle and about one-fifth of the usual quota of officers from other organizations. I slept to my heart's content and had one of the best Thanksgiving dinners that I had ever tasted. Our company had 225 pounds of turkey and all the accessories to go with it. Our mess sergeant, who was one of the cleanest cut lads I had ever seen in the service, was also the best cook in the regiment. Sgt. Turner had worked much of the night trying to cook our many turkeys in his very primitive oven; he fixed up two kinds of desserts, he made delicious oyster dressing, and my platoon decorated the mess hall with holly, which grew in abundance there. Shinkle and I were the only two officers to enjoy the feast, but we did it justice. He and I were the long distance eaters of the company, and we went at our gastronomic problem just as if it were a final test for supremacy to be decided then. We came out about even.

Sgt. Turner did have his faults however, and those shortcomings almost cost us our Thanksgiving feast. Liquor was difficult to acquire at Quantico, but Sgt. Turner found and consumed some lemon extract on Wednesday night. In the middle of the night he decided that, in his words, "I want to scalp a nigger." [Editors Note: Being set over 100 years ago,

42

some words within this work may be offensive to some readers. However, they have been left as is for their historical context.] He stripped to the waist and went out with a butcher knife. Only one permanent building stood on the base, and behind it Turner was chasing some poor soul around the pool when the officer of the guard came around on his inspection tour. As soon as Sgt. Turner saw the officer of the guard, he was very military and immediately saluted, but the guard put him in the brig anyway. Well, I was still a very green lieutenant, and my experienced sergeant was gone for the holiday. I did not know what to do. But my men, the old noncoms, found Turner's uniform and ironed his khaki pants. They even smuggled a razor into the brig, so when Turner appeared before the Colonel, he was a perfect Marine. Our 6th Marine Regiment Detachment Commander was old Lt. Colonel Harry Lee, USMC, a handsome man, of the Virginia Lee family. As the emergency ended, Sgt. Turner was only reprimanded for being off post in a non-regulation uniform, and our properly cooked Thanksgiving dinner was saved.

2ndLt. Neil F. Dougherty, USMC, one of the lieutenants who was instructing in the second Officer's School, and I went to Washington D.C. on December 1. As usual we did not have such a good time. It was my opinion that Washington was one of the sleepiest, coldest, inhospitable places I had ever visited. We went to a vaudeville show in the afternoon, to a movie after supper, and to the Chevy Chase Country Club in the evening for a dance. It was a rather crusty method by which we got to that dance. About four weeks before, when we had a little dance after a vaudeville performance in the Y.M.C.A., I met, very casually, a young lady named Tuttle, who was one of the elite in Washington. I danced a couple of times with her, but we were not especially congenial. I had forgotten all about the incident until this day. As Dougherty and I were going into lunch, and as we were feeling in fine fettle, we were giving all the girls we saw the once over. Just outside of our cafe, I spied a nice looking girl sitting in an electric car with her mother. Much to my surprise she bowed and spoke most cordially. I was too astonished to do anything at the time, but I realized that before me stood Miss Tuttle. So when Dougherty and I were seated inside the cafe, I thought that here was an opportunity to find something to do in the evening. So out again I went to the car, and by maneuvering as skillfully as I could, I got an invitation for Dougherty and myself to go to the Country Club that evening. It was rather a shameless thing to do, but we didn't care.

I had an engagement to go out walking with a young lady, Miss Byington, one afternoon in early December; she was the sister-in-law of one of our majors in the artillery, Major Ross E. Rowell. I had met him and her through Captain Messersmith, who was a very good friend of the family. The major, his wife and Miss Byington had been camping out, more or less, there in Quantico ever since the major was ordered to the base, and I had the pleasure of seeing them quite frequently. They all went up to Washington D.C. on the same train in which Dougherty and I rode, and there we made arrangements for our afternoon walk.

We had a fine stroll enlivened by the presence of the 78th Company mascot, our little bull terrier Dixie, who was a great favorite of the ladies. We had tea in the Rowell apartment after our walk, and later had supper with the Major over in his company mess hall. I was quick to write my parents warning them not to place too much thought about me falling in love "for many a moon."

During the next few weeks I chanced to meet several fellows that I knew at Wentworth; one being Pvt. Robert C. Clore, 17th Co., 5th Marine Regiment, a good type of Marine. Pvt. Donald D. Shakespeare, Supply Company., 5th Marine Regiment, was another. As a cadet, he had won the athletic and shooting medal. I was very much surprised to see him as I had heard that he was in an Army camp in the West. My father had sent him an offer to get into the officers' reserve of the Marine Corps at the same time Mordecai and I went in. But Shakespeare was intending at that time to go into the army. So he turned the offer down. He became impatient over the delay in the other proposition though and enlisted as a private in the Marines. I would have liked very much to have had him transferred to my company, as he was a fine looking lad and had had experience in the military dope. But he was in another regiment and such a thing would be impossible.

We were still without definite information about our departure, but there were persistent rumors afloat which had a more convincing source than our former ones. One sergeant and one private from our company were invited to take Thanksgiving dinner with the Major General Commandant, and they reported that the Commandant told them that the 2nd Battalion would leave before the 15th of December. The betting was growing brisk among the officers that we should be leaving before that time. But, as I said before, I believed nothing until we actually got our orders, and even then would retain my doubts until we had boarded our transport.

A number of us were able to get leave for the Christmas holidays, and I returned to my family in Lexington. My father was not in the best of health at the time and I found myself quite concerned for him, and the regular operation of Wentworth Military Academy. I suggested that certain changes should be made in order to relieve my father of the burden. I had learned that I could handle the work at Wentworth very effectively after my Quantico training. I hoped that I would be able to come back and do something of the sort and run things with my brother Sandy. But then again, I was enjoying the Marine Corps and thought I might never leave.

I had to return to Quantico by the 1st of January. My return trip was more pleasant than the trip going home; I made good connections all the way and secured berths both nights. The only inconveniences I had to put up with were caused by a scarcity of dining cars along the route. We had to go without food from breakfast until supper. But, I realized that fasting was a good thing now and then and I didn't suffer much. I picked up a touch of flu at home; I coughed some during the nights en route, but by New Year's night I slept soundly and coughed none. I did not want to jeopardize my position and took my medicine religiously. 2ndLt. Lieutenant Paul S. Taylor, USMC, had to get an extension of leave on account of the same trouble, and he would not return until he had recovered. Also 2ndLt. John G. "Jack" Schneider, a St. Joseph boy, who was a lieutenant in our battalion, contracted a case of Scarlet Fever while he was at home, so I felt pretty lucky to have gotten off as easily as I did.

On the morning of January 2, the Major Holcomb told us that again our departure had been delayed by an accident to the boat which was to have taken us. He said that we would probably leave about the end of the month, instead of the middle. We were all thoroughly disgusted. During this period, everyone was as busy as the proverbial cat on the hot tin roof, and in addition to the regular routine, we had been having a special course under some English officers.

The old major, not to be outdone, also decided that he would hold school, and much in the manner of my V.M.I. instructors at Wentworth in the days gone by, he kept a book open and we recited from it. He knew little or no more than we did about the stuff, and it was considerably a joke, but it pleased the old boy, and he thought he was accomplishing a great deal in those classes. This studying became the regular routine of work in addition to the usual drills. The poor platoon leaders caught the brunt of this added work, and we hardly had time to steal an occasional bath.

It was a shame that in the Marine Corps the officers got as little instruction as we did. One of the Canadian officers, a former Brit, who was rather frank in his utterances, was said to have remarked to the Major General Commandant that he had never seen such a fine body of enlisted men in his life, and that he had never seen such inefficient training given to any troops. He was partly right, too. The policy of the Corps had been that of a bunch of old fogies who thought they knew everything, and no one outside had any right or any excuse to instruct or criticize them. The organization was much like that of a snobbish fraternity, the members of which thought they were better than anyone else. Nevertheless, I will say that we had as good or better discipline than any organization which I knew about, and I still believe that is nine-tenths of the battle.

On the weekend of January 12 and 13, I made off to Richmond one last time, and not with any matrimonial intentions, as my father supposed. As usual, I had a grand and glorious time, which I needed badly. The Munces had received three letters from George, who crossed with the machine gun battalion, and I listened to the reading of them with considerable interest. It seemed that the Marines had finally been mobilized across the ocean, and although the censor was very strict on the letters which I read, nevertheless, I could read a good deal between the lines.

Finally on January 15, Major Holcomb definitely informed us that we would shove off by the end of that week, and we had some reliable informal information that the exact time would be Saturday morning, the 19th. To say that we were pleased mildly expresses it. We started packing up in earnest, and everything in the usual routine was knocked off by Wednesday in order for us to prepare for our departure. I shipped home a suitcase of surplus stuff as I wanted to travel as light as possible. The Major arranged for us to draw our advance pay and to have our pay accounts transferred to Battalion headquarters; the Adjutant went to Philadelphia to arrange for our mess, and to find out the particulars of how much room would be allowed us aboard. I looked forward to trying out Dr. Paine's sea-sickness pills. The men of course got wind of the possible departure, and there was considerable expectancy on their part, although we tried not to let them know any more than was absolutely necessary.

As promised, that Saturday morning at 4:00 a.m, we rose from our makeshift bunks and did the final touching up around quarters. The day before, we had packed nearly everything on box cars; so very little work was required. The Major was exceedingly anxious for us to make our departure a model of orderliness and precision, and although my experiences along such lines were limited, it seemed to me that we did remarkably well. We had muster formation at 5:30 a.m. The Captain went through the vacated quarters to see that everything was cleaned up and that the bunks were left in perfect order. Then with packs on our back, in full marching order we moved down to the station. The stars were out, but there was no moon, and only the street lamps gave us light. It was a case of folding out tents and silently stealing away. But when we arrived at the station, we found that somebody had routed out the band, which, shivering, tried its best to render us some cheerful music. The men didn't need much cheering up however; they were all very much elated at the prospect of leaving.

Our train pulled up only 10 minutes late, and we piled into the coaches previously designated for us. My platoon was fortunate in drawing a coach just behind the engine, with plenty of steam heat turned on. We also had enough seats to allow three men to four seats. I learned that all of the rear coaches were inadequately heated, but we traveled deluxe.

Despite the heavy schedule, I found time to write home often during those days. In my last letter to my father before sailing for France, I wrote:

"Now I do not want you and Mother to worry about me in the least. I want you to feel that all of the teachings which you have given me are not wasted. I shall, with God's help, lead as clean a life when I go across, as I have done in this country, and I can truthfully say that there is mighty little which I have done to be ashamed of. And as long as I can live clean there is nothing else to be afraid of as I see it. I know that while

you and Mother know that I am living straight, you will not worry, and with the memory of you and Mother, and your prayers behind me, I feel absolutely safe. There may never be any call for me to go near the trenches, and I may never have to do any fighting; but if I do, and I can not but wish that I get the chance, I hope that I may prove a good soldier of my country."

4

OVER THERE

The battalion's movement overseas was incremental. The 1st Battalion sailed on Sunday, September 23, 1917. The 3rd Battalion pushed off on Wednesday (Halloween), October 31, 1917 and finally, on January 19, 1918, we traveled by train to League Island Navy Yard, Philadelphia, Pennsylvania, where we boarded the U.S. Naval Transport, U.S.S. *Henderson*. The old timers knew why we were last. Maj. Holcomb's wife was due to deliver a son, and he had enough influence to ensure that we were the last ones to sail. Later in life, when Holcomb was the Corps Commandant, I happened to be in Washington D.C. at a military school's meeting when they gave him his first parade at the Marine Barracks, Washington D.C. He said to me, "Sandy, come over here and meet the reason why we were the last ones." He then introduced me to his son, Frank.

The U.S.S. *Henderson* was a very unusual ship. The Marine Corps took possession of it when the United States believed in the Monroe Doctrine. The ship was fixed up to house a whole battalion.

From Philadelphia, we sailed to New York and went ashore. I was the only one within the group who had ever been to New York City, and I directed five of the boys to "Risenwebbers," a dance pavilion where a fine orchestra was playing. At the table next to us sat a man and two girls. He asked one of them to dance. I made some signals to the unaccompanied girl. She indicated that she was willing, so we started to dance, but the *maître d'* came over and broke us up. My compatriots started to come to my rescue, but I shushed them down, and soon the man and his girl came back. The man called me over and told me that he was responsible for the bouncer telling me to shove off, since he wanted to meet me first. He had been dancing with his fiancée, and I had been dancing with her sister. After this somewhat rocky start, I had a pleasant evening dancing with this girl, and she then adopted me as her war work. While I was overseas she occasionally sent me candy, letters, and copies of the *New York Times*. I saw her after the war, and we danced to the music of a very well-known orchestra. This fair haired young man from Missouri was not amused when she informed me that she had gone to a fortune teller who told her that she was going to marry a man from the West who was blond.

On January 24, we sailed from New York Harbor in a convoy escorted by destroyers. We boarded our transport at about 3:00 p.m. on January 24, got settled as soon as we could, but left most of the baggage to be moved later as the box cars had not come alongside. At supper time the Captain of the ship announced that all but two officers from each company might go ashore. All of us wanted to; so we cut for the privilege and I lost. It was up to me therefore, to stay with the ship and super-intend the storing of the baggage. It was a rather tough propo-sition for me, but the Captain gave me a few pointers, and I tackled the job. All the baggage had to be brought aboard over a single gangplank, wide enough for two to stand abreast on, and with 1000 men all trying to work at once, it was some job to keep the stuff separate, and to get it on board at all. The heavy baggage had to be brought up by cranes. When it was ready to be hoisted, I went up to the Officer of the Deck, and, as per instructions of the Captain, I said, "Sir the baggage is alongside, will you please rig the boom." I had no idea what the boom was, but my bluff got away, and a big derrick, which I presumed to be the boom, was put in operation. It was not until about 9:00 p.m. that we finally got everything set, and then we had to leave some of it out on the deck to be made fast.

The ship which we were on was designed by Marine Officers, who had in mind the comfort of themselves and men; so we were housed especially well, with all of the modern "inconveniences," as my father referred to them. Every officer, even brand new lieutenants like me, had a stateroom for himself. I had a little stateroom with mirrors, lights, 4 of them, a bureau with a desk in it which pulled out like a drawer, a washbasin which folded up against the wall, and a good bunk. It was surprising to see how comfortable such a small space could be made. Besides, every two of the officers had a Negro boy who tended to all their wants, and there was a bell right there for me to ring whenever I wanted my boy's services. He didn't wait for, or expect, a tip either. Then we had a big roomy dining room, and the service we got would make the Ritz Carlton management green with envy. Between meal times we congregated in the wardroom to play cards, read, or listen to the phonograph. At Quantico, a group of congenial souls played poker, and the same group got together on the ship. No effort was made to keep troops from gambling. Most of the time I played gin rummy and was lucky enough to garner some pocket money. The windows looked forward and since they were on the upper deck, we got a good view of the seascape.

Our duties aboard ship were far from exciting. We had to conduct a lookout drill for our men during the first two days aboard, and since we had actually put to sea, we had to practice what we learned. A ship, in those days especially, had to have exceedingly sharp eyes. So at night there were sixteen men constantly searching the sea for anything suspicious. They were all provided with binoculars, and to each was assigned a small sector to search thoroughly. These men were relieved every hour, so that at all times there were fresh men on the job sweeping the entire circle with their glasses. Every object seen was reported whether it was a log, a piece of wreckage or even a bird on the water. We reported these objects to the fire control officer, who was constantly practicing his gun crews in training their sights on these targets. During the day there were 25 of these lookouts, always on the job, along with three officers in charge of them. We had to stand a two or four hour watch every day, which wasn't so bad.

On January 24, I received my order to report for watch on the fore-top. So at the proper time I went out to find my post. I had no idea what the fore-top was, but I quickly deduced that it had to be one of the two masts on the ships. I was to climb to the crow's nest with two enlisted men and use binoculars to look out for submarines or anything else that seemed suspicious. I asked an old Marine, one of the captains with whom I had played some poker, which was the fore-top. After he told me, I climbed straight up the mast. Now on this ship the fore-top lookout was about 80 feet high; it was the crow's nest on the forward mast. There were shrouds on each side of the mast, and it was an easy matter to swarm up them. But this first day, I didn't see them, and instead I simply climbed straight up the mast. When I had almost reached the top, I realized the rungs did not go as far as the crow's nest. I should have climbed the shrouds to reach it. The shrouds were only about three feet away and I was tempted to leap across, but I felt as if I was a mile high and the swaying of the ship did nothing to bolster my confidence. So I had an argument between my laziness and my cowardice as to whether to take a chance and swing over or go back down and climb up the shrouds. My laziness finally won; I lunged across and survived.

Afterward, I was rather proud of myself. But my knees were quite shaky when I finally made it, and it was a grand and glorious feeling when I was safely in the nest. Marines, of course, were supposed to know how to handle these predicaments, but I had never seen the ocean. I had never sailed on anything larger than Lake Michigan and the Missouri River.

The first few days we were fortunate in having very calm weather and smooth seas. But when I woke on the morning of the 26th, I could feel the ship bouncing around like a cork. There were about two or three inches of water on the floor of my room, and I watched my shoes and socks swimming all around. The black boys were busy scooping all the water out on deck; so, thought I, we must be having some weather. But I found that someone had turned the faucet of a shower bath when the water wasn't running on our deck, and during the night it had flooded everything. We were pitching and rolling so badly by then though, that it wouldn't surprise me if water had come hurtling through my port.

On Friday the 25th, I went up in the fore-top again, but on the 26th I took my tour of duty as deck officer, in charge of the lower lookouts. It was rather a bad tour too. Major Holcomb had issued an order stating that seasickness would not be allowed aboard ship; however a good many of the men were growing green around the gills and feeling as sick as possible. But they were made to take their turns just the same. It wasn't safe to walk around below the lookout houses because you knew not what might come down upon you. I felt rather mean when I made one little Marine, who was so sick he could hardly move, clean up his look-out post which he had made almost untenable. But no one was excused from anything on account of "mal de mer." Our black mess boys were the one exception. Most were dropping out, one by one, since it was not deemed advisable to have them continue their duties. Our service likewise deteriorated, because we could have no more dishes on the table than we could hold on to. Imagine all of us sitting with our legs wrapped around the table supports, a glass of water clasped desperately in one hand and a plate balanced in the other, snatching a bite as our food goes by. At every roll a bunch of silverware or china went crashing down somewhere, and waiters were just as apt to spill our food down the back of our necks as to place it in front of us on the tables.

My boy was an old Pullman porter, and he could clean up my room in about two seconds. He was an African aristocrat as many Pullman porters were, and he confided to me that if he had known that such "common niggers" were accepted, he would never have enlisted in the Navy. [Editors Note: Being set over 100 years ago, some words within this work may be offensive to some readers. However, they have been left as is for their historical context.] I suppose that on account of his railroad experience, he was used to being bumped around; so he did not succumb.

I was anxious to see how I could walk when I got on land again, as I cultivated a pretty good pair of sea legs. Much contrary to my anticipations, I did not get a bit sick, and we had some pretty rough weather too. But I pitied the poor enlisted men. They were jammed up so tight down below that when we wanted to inspect their compartments, we had to run them all up on deck. Their bunks were arranged in three tiers, and there was barely room for two people to pass between the tiers. During the rougher weather, it was an awful sight to behold down below. About three quarters of them wished they were dead; some said that they didn't intend to go back to America unless they could fly. But even the sickest of them could always get up courage to laugh at the other guy, and not a one failed to come up at the proper times. Of the officers, only three or four were at all sick, and none of them badly, except the chaplain, a little fat Catholic.

On the morning of February 1, I went up in the fore-top again. By then, it gave me a thrill to go up there in such rough weather. The boat rolled so much that the lookouts were careened out right over the water, and it was rather ticklish business climbing up there with the wind whipping our clothes and waving our shrouds around. We were rather lucky to get used to going aloft in smooth weather so that by then we did not mind the roughness so much. We had some other transports in our little fleet, and there was one lone battleship convoying us. We arrived in the war zone that day, and that night we doubled the number of lookouts; also we took extra precautions concerning lights, and the carrying of life preservers. Ever since we left the States, we closed up all our port holes, in order to expose no light at night. Consequently I suffocated after sun down, because closing the ports shut out air as well as shutting in light. To exacerbate matters, my stateroom happened to be over the "Jack of the Dust," as we Marines called the bakery. At times my room was so hot that I could not put my feet on the floor. Finally one night I took my bedding roll right out on the deck and turned in. We were in a latitude north of New York in the middle of winter, but I had to throw off all but one blanket during the first of the night. The moon was peeping out through the clouds, and the waves were swishing along the sides of the ship, and I just lay awake for a long time enjoying it all.

When we went through the war zone, we spent all the time right up on our toes. Early on the morning of the 4th, an additional convoy composed of speedy little destroyers came out to meet us. I knew that it would have given my father a thrill to see these trim little craft go skimming and careening over the waves. They were capable of doing 33 knots an hour, and for a ship of any size that was pretty good. They were camouflaged thoroughly, and there was considerable rivalry between the lookouts to see them first, for we knew about when to expect them. With the destroyers' escort, we put on full speed and humped right along. We kept our life preservers on all the time, and at short intervals we all turned out for an abandon-ship drill. It became quite a nuisance to hear all the bells go clanging at any time, and then to turn out on the double to answer the summons.

The morning of the 5th was our most dangerous period,

because a wily submarine was fond of working in the early dawn, and we were getting near to our destination. So, to be prepared for the worst, they made us all turn out at daybreak and stand around on deck in order to have a better chance if anything should turn up. There was considerable excitement for a minute or two when a slow speaking lookout reported a "Submarine destroyer." The lad who received the report shouted "Submarine" at the top of his voice as soon as the lookout got the first word out of his mouth. The Major promptly put these two out of a job.

We came through without any excitement at all. We stood by to enter our dock as soon as the authorities permitted us to do so, but we had to wait a couple of more days before we were allowed to set our conquering foot upon the land. We eagerly awaited anything that might turn up.

5

TRAINING IN FRANCE

The U.S.S. *Henderson* docked at St. Nazaire, France, on Friday, February 8, 1918. We immediately went ashore, and one of our first introductions to the French was in the men's room, where we were shocked to find women cleaning up while we answered the calls of nature. We left the seacoast after a very short delay and came inland without much of an idea as to where we were going or how far. We didn't travel in exactly deluxe fashion, but at any rate, I thoroughly enjoyed the trip, especially during daylight.

From St. Nazaire we entrained and headed for the tiny French village of Damblain. When we arrived there to spend the night, we were greeted by some of the Marines who had preceded us. 2ndLt. William Ashurst, USMC, was among those present. Our first stop was only temporary however, and the morning after our arrival we hiked cross country about 4 1/2 miles to our billets in the larger town of Robecourt, where we spent five weeks of additional training. We were far behind the front lines and the atmosphere was completely peaceful. There we were introduced to rural France.

To me, France seemed sort of a country of contrasts, some places being marvels of scrupulous cleanliness, and other places and all the people just the opposite. But on our travels the friendliness of the people, the beauty of the landscape, the absence of smoke, and the usual dirty atmosphere one has to contend with while traveling in the States, made the trip a real pleasure.

Luckily, my old friend 2ndLt. George Munce, USMC, was also billeted in the same village. Several others of the officers in George's company (73rd Machine Gun Co.) were also good friends of mine, and one of them, Capt. Roy C. Swink, USMC, arranged for Shinkle and me to move into the room adjoining theirs in one of the pretentious houses of the town.

There was an American-made wood stove in our room, but the thing smoked us out because the stove pipe didn't fit; so I gave it to part of my platoon which was billeted in rather frigid quarters. Our company had no government billets, but was quartered here and there throughout town in barns and houses not in use. Sometimes the enlisted men were billeted in the lofts of barns with the horses and cows below. These accommodations were rough but not uncomfortable. I had trouble getting my men located at first, but finally I placed them all in adequate places. In one barn, members of my platoon slept above the stall occupied by the village stallion.

It was a quite a spectacle when a mare was to be bred to the stallion. A little boy would assist, going around underneath the situation. It was a regular social event with everyone in town, women and men, boys and girls, there. The officers likewise were put at the mercy of the populace, but care was taken to give them plenty of room and supposedly heat. An old mademoiselle owned the house in which we stayed, and there was nothing in her power which she wouldn't do for us. Every morning she had *"de l'ean chaud"* for us, and she was always seeking to help us in any way. We had French furnishings altogether in one room, the quaintest furniture I ever saw; but the beds were the most peculiar items. They had two mattresses on them with a thickness of about two feet. On top of them in addition to the regular covers, there was sort of a huge pillow filled with eider down I presume, about 4 feet square; we called them bomb-proofs. Then overhead, we had canopies like those I used to look at in palace interiors in an old European picture book of my father's. We also had the only piano in town, but it had no two keys which were in tune.

Our town was well off the railroad, and I was told that the inhabitants were well on the road to starvation before the Americans arrived. They seemed to be duly grateful, although they did charge us rather high prices for what little we could buy from them.

We had rather chilly weather when we arrived, but there was not so much rain as I had expected. Even though it didn't rain much, the ground always appeared to be soaked, and whenever it thawed, there was a lot of mud to contend with. We did have rain or snow or both every day for a week in late February, and as we carried out our schedules just the same, it was very difficult to keep our clothes in shape. But no matter what happened, all we could do was say *"c'est la guerre"* and put up with it.

Our schedule was one of seven days. I had never worked so hard for one day at home as I had every day for those first few weeks in France. And after our field work was finished we had a great many duties in the billets. Censoring the mail from my platoon was by no means the least of these duties, because the many college and high school boys in our company grasped every opportunity to write their girls at home, and on every holiday, most of my time was consumed in censoring. Luckily for this phase of my work, holidays were few and far between, and most of us were too fagged to do anything. It still seemed that my men wrote about three letters per man per day. We were not allowed to write our location, any particulars of our training, or any dates of happenings. On a holiday it was not uncommon for me to censor a hundred letters at a sitting and I became rather brain-weary as a result of reading so much drivel. Nearly all the boys said practically the same thing, but when I glanced back over my own effort, I couldn't say mine was much different.

I had also been trying to keep up my correspondence with my family and friends most religiously. I had intended to write very frequently from that side, but did well to get in a weekly letter. Spare moments to answer letters were "conspicuous by their absence," as one of my men wrote. I wasn't receiving much mail in reply, especially in the first few weeks. I hoped that the mail system would improve for us, but I understood that it was usually rather eccentric in the case of troops newly arrived. I usually received my mail about six weeks after it had been mailed in the U.S. Mail was at an exceedingly high premium over there; "more precious than much fine gold." When I received from the U.S. my hometown newspapers, the *Lexington Intelligencer* or the *Wentworth Trumpeter*, I read them through carefully, from the date to the "Watch this space" advertisement.

I had been trying to learn a little French but unfortunately wasn't getting as much practice as I had wanted. When I was constantly with the company from 5:30 a.m. or thereabouts, until after supper in the evening, I was unable to stir up any interesting acquaintances among the natives. We were out all day, and in the evenings our time was completely taken up with military studies and other tasks. Therefore the only chance I had to "parler" were occasional chats with our landlady, and believe me I did well to catch the general topic of conversation, and not much else. We had rough going of it, as she talked too fast for me to catch much, and my Parisian accent and original idioms were rather bewildering to her. I knew more French when I was in college the year before than I knew then. My orderly, Swedish by birth, but with more free time than I, made much better progress.

At Robecourt, we went through arduous training consisting of practice hikes, more trench digging, bomb throwing, and standing by all night in the trenches. The weather worked against us, and the great deal of mud impeded our progress. Most of the training was done in daylight, and at night we went back to shelter. On one of those days our mascot Dixie, the bulldog, took out after Major Thomas Holcomb's horse. He and the adjutant were the only ones who were mounted during these exercises. The horse took off at a full gallop with our battalion commander astride. We thought we were going to lose Dixie over that incident. Fortunately we did not.

My company was issued cheaply manufactured French automatic rifles known as the *chauchat*. These weapons looked as if they were made out of cigar boxes and tin cans, and we had an awful time making our men carry them. A man shooting one almost was in as much danger as anyone out in front being shot at. The big machine guns were issued only to the machine gun company, and we were not given the M1918 Browning Automatic Rifles to replace the *chauchats* until the very end of the war.

The weather conditions were such that George Washington at Valley Forge had nothing on us. Believe me the knitted goods which I got from home were vastly appreciated and in some cases at first, under-rated. Lyman, my old weather-beaten gunnery sergeant, scoffed when we were issued knitted helmets, wristlets and sweaters back at Quantico, but he told me, after our arrival in France, that "it was the best joke he had ever had played on him, and he'd like a few more like it." A friend of mine knitted me a cap, and I used it just as and where it was intended to be used in the abominable weather. Those confounded newspaper cartoonists may have slung derision at the knitters, but nobody there did so. We thanked the Lord that somebody loved us enough to make us stuff.

I also had monthly allotments sent to my Dad, as I had arranged with the paymaster before my departure. I wished that I had made a larger one, because there was no use whatsoever of money over there, and I couldn't even get to a bank to put in what I had accumulated. I thought that what I saved out would be necessary for my upkeep, but I couldn't have had a liberal week-end in the States on what I'd spent in my first month in France, and I left March's pay with the paymaster, who had arrived so late that another pay day was due. I felt like a bloated bond holder as a result.

After we had spent a number of weeks in rigorous training and had become hardened, we earned some leisure time. The gang which had formerly played penny ante poker back in Quantico assembled in one of those villages. We had too many for a poker game, but someone had a pair of dice. I had never shot craps in my life but I knew the theory, and I had been a little fortunate at gin rummy on the ship going over. We all had some spare change and few outlets to spend it. At the end of the evening my pocket was filled with French francs, which meant little more than cigar coupons to me at the time. Before another weekend, when I might have lost it all, we received orders for the front and were instructed to take not more than a hundred francs on our person. So after translating the francs into dollars, I found myself with $650 worth of money orders, which equaled about four months' pay. I knew this would cause some question by my father if I sent them to him. Instead, I addressed the letter containing the money orders to my oldest brother Ovid, who I thought was still in Chicago, and asked him to purchase some Liberty Bonds. He had then become an ordained minister, but he knew the frailty of youth and would not publicize my gambling winnings.

We moved up as a Division to the front lines near Verdun, France on St. Patrick's Day, March 17, 1918. Our destination was Camp L'Eveche, which we later nicknamed "Neverest." The camp was located in the Verdun Sector, where the combined losses of Germans and French totaled 600,000 during the largest engagement of the war. Verdun was rather quiet by the time we arrived, and we were able to go in and visit the city.

The Germans had had quite a salient there and had caused considerable damage, but they had not taken the town.

Major Thomas Holcomb, USMC, our battalion commander, came out one night shortly after we had arrived at L'Eveche to inspect my platoon. The French had previously occupied the trenches we were inhabiting, and they had made their bunks out of two by fours and chicken wire, and had left grenades, ammunition, and other supplies in every nook and cranny. Of course, Major Holcomb had to find something to criticize, so he zeroed in on the mess the French had left for us. The Major's criticisms insulted my platoon GySgt. George H. Lyman. As I was coming back around a corner I heard Sergeant Lyman talking to another sergeant, and, referring to Holcomb, he said, "He ain't worth a cock full of cold piss." I had never heard such a vile expression in my entire life. He was taking up for me of course, but I am surely glad the Major did not hear him.

At L'Eveche we rotated between front line duty, where we dug trenches, and reserve, serving in support of those who replaced us. Our front line assignment once was in a tiny town out in the middle of a marsh. Deep mud was everywhere, and we were ordered to move back and forth only at night, using a road protected by *cheveaux de frise*, the barbed wire entanglements found all over the Western Front. We spent 55 days in this comparatively quiet sector, where by mutual consent neither side did much shooting. Rumor had it that a one-legged German in the opposing trench went down the line at 5 o'clock every evening and fired a burst of rounds from each machine gun before going to sleep. We did get used to hearing an occasional bullet directed our way, but during all that time only one 78th Company man, Pvt. Raymond Crow, USMCR, was killed at Verdun on Friday, April 26, 1918.

In the first week of April, we were doing no hiking or drilling at all, and for a change, I became master of my time. We had finally become somewhat used to the rigorous schedule. I shouldn't have thought a year before that I could have stood walking 20 miles on a hot day, and carrying everything on my back that would serve me as bedding and clothing for a couple of months, not to speak of arms, ammunition and a two days' ration of food. But that was what we had to do, and besides, I often had to carry a couple of rifles and an extra fifteen pounds of ammunition for some of my men who were even more heavily loaded than I. But I was a regular truck horse by then, and it was an old story with me to pick up my bed and walk. I often longed for the old fox trot days, but after all, this was the best game in the world, and I'd rather have been there than anywhere else. It was all in a day's work there, and it was surprising to see what a man could do when he had to. Besides, I was with the Marine Corps, which was the top notch organization of the A.E.F., and I didn't believe there were any better men in the Allied Armies. That might sound a little "higgaty" but it's still my honest belief. Despite everything, I had the happy-go-luckiest bunch of boys in my platoon that I had ever seen, and we would come in singing from the hardest day's hike a man was ever intended to make. And I would rather have been right there with them than anywhere else in the world. I knew that this life would be the making of a lot of men. It was rather funny how philosophical we became.

Near Mont-sous-le Cote, France at that time, I was in command of what was once a small village, uninhabited then, except by rats and certain other "varmints," and my platoon of Marines. They ought to have called us Maroons though, because nobody could visit there or depart during daylight. We had to sleep all day, stay under cover, then come out and stand to during the night, having breakfast just after nightfall, dinner at 11:30 p.m. and supper about 7 a.m. We burned no fires at all during daylight. The afternoon of April 3, some of my men were slightly indiscreet and began chopping wood out in the open. About an hour later I received the following message over the buzzer: "What damage from the shells this afternoon." It was great sport, but I hoped my luck continued.

My abode there, though not quite Blackstone in its appointments, was the most comfortable I had had since I had struck that God forsaken country. I had a small room lined with tar paper, to keep the rats out, and heated by a diminutive stove; my orderly stole enough wood to keep me supplied with warmth and warm water, to toast my bread, warm my coffee and fry my bacon. I got a candle every night to light up with, and the carpenter fixed me a four poster made of two-by-fours and some chicken wire. So I lived in luxury.

Extremely poor rations were given us when we arrived at L'Eveche. The bread was moldy, and we did not get very much. But that soon changed. One night by some unknown streak of luck, I got five turkeys, cranberry sauce, potatoes and some dates, which I bought for the platoon from the Y.M.C.A. We had only an open fire and some large kettles to cook on, but my mess men fixed up the stuff pretty well. I can still envision us feasting on this chow about midnight. We usually lived on stew (known as slum), canned "bill," and hard tack, with an occasional slab of bacon. I once overheard one of my men remark that he was going to carve some "heliogryphics" on a piece of hardtack and mail it to his girl. But like everything else there, it was all right when you got used to it. We occasionally got jams, and we nearly always had fresh bread.

When provisions came in from the Y.M.C.A., I often bought some jam and cookies. These little extras which we could buy were certainly a blessing. The men could get smokes, which next to chow, were the most important item of our provisions. When the men got enough to eat and smoke, they could go through anything. A few nights in March at the time of year for the "passover," we were all given unleavened bread. Around that time an order came around to the company commanders to find out how many Jews of their command wished the unleavened bread for the fast period. Of the ten whom he questioned, nine said they wanted it if they received the regular allowance of rations in addition. The tenth, one Isidore Greenberg, chose the orthodox bread unconditionally; the Captain made him a corporal.

We were not in the enormous battle in process in early April, although I wished we had been. The French had been departing in a steady stream for the scene of greater action. There was constant need of soldiers and more soldiers. It was certainly the biggest game in the world, and I was only glad that I could go through hardships for such a righteous cause. My men had just the right kind of spirit, and I thanked my stars many times to have gotten with such an aggregation. We were always cheerful and feeling fine. I was never in better shape myself, and nearly all the old friends I met looked fat and frisky.

We had been supplied with different colored flares and sirens to indicate a gas attack. Once we were out digging trenches when I thought I heard a siren go off, so I had the platoon put on their gas masks. The "siren" turned out to be a mule braying, much to my embarrassment. Actually, our position's elevation and the wind made it nearly impossible for the Germans to gas us. Our trenches were laid out in a haphazard design, paralleling the front with traverses connecting the rear trenches with the front ones. Some were shallow, but most were over six feet deep.

As April wore on, it was move, move, move for us, and our hours were so irregular that I had been unable to formulate any system. Nearly everything we did was carried on at night; we marched, worked and sometimes ate at night. It seemed perfectly natural for me to be up and doing something in the middle of the night. Our Company had been to the front lines in three different places, and trench life was rapidly becoming second nature to us. We had been far more comfortable in the trenches near Ronvaux than anywhere else, and as for my part I preferred it to other duty. Of course we had to shave and wash in a cup of water; we had to poke around in inky darkness— everyone had a cane to guide himself; we had to live on half cooked food some of the time, but we always got excellent bread, and we never got used to the whizz-bang of the shells. But our duties were not arduous, unless particularly bad weather prevailed; we got our mail regularly, and we learned to sleep comfortably anywhere.

One night in late April, I jotted down a poem which I sent to a girl, and I read it to my orderly, a young Norwegian from North Dakota named Pvt. Melvin O. Olson. He was much impressed and asked permission to copy it. I let him do so and he sent it to the editor of his home paper for publication. For his preamble to the editor he wrote: "...Someone has said that in the springtime a young man's fancy turns lightly to love and poetry, hence it is natural that these thoughts of mine written to the rhythm of booming guns should find expression in verse for those back home who have more than an idle curiosity to know how this life appeals to us, I submit the following to you for publication." We laughed a good deal over his deception, and I kidded him a lot about it. This is the "pome."

> Tonight I'm off, no work for me,
> So here upon the bunk I be,
> And having read a little verse,
> I thought that I could do no worse
> Than certain others. So here goes
> A few mild plaints upon the woes
> A line or two anent the joys
> Of course they like to call our boys
> Somewhere in France—a dreadful place
> Believe me dear, sans e'en a trace
> Of pleasure that we used to know.
> We can't attend the movie show
> Nor shake a mean knee to the jazz
> Nor note what taking ways she has
> With those great big brown eyes of hers,
> Instead we're cussing out those curs,
> The boches and stumbling round in slime,

Up to our necks long after time
That honest folks should be in bed,
A never ending rain o'erhead,
A mud filled trench beneath our feet,
Which we're supposed to make so neat
And dry, that e'en the Colonel's eye
Can find no fault. And so we try
To clean the darn thing up with pick
And shovel, but we get so sick
Of sticking to the dirty job,
That something very like a sob,
Escapes from some poor kid too young
To stand the gaff. The sergeant's tongue
Cuts in to goad on one who's quit
Who's got the brawn but not the grit
To stick. And so it gets my goat,
To read some dainty perfumed note
From o'er the seas which goes like this:
"Dear Mac: Life must be full of bliss,
"For you brave boys who're over there,
"In sunny France, and I declare,
"I'll bet you're kidding all those dames,
"Those chic m'am selles with frilly names
"And strutting round in khaki clad
"And showing what a handsome lad
"You think you are." But here gee whiz,
For us to get along with all,
The hardships that our country's call
Has forced on us. They even close
Down vaudeville and the picture shows,
Two times a week to save the fuel.
You must admit how very cruel
That is; and if I had my say
You bet there'd be no war to-day.

I became a regular cave dweller in late April. This time my dugout had a brownstone front. My platoon's dugout was at the base of an old quarry cliff, and mine was half way up the face. The rock was of sandstone, and it was cracked all the way up in one place. The Frenchies entered there and hollowed out my abode. I was as safe as a bug in a rug, in a solid rock dugout built or rather hollowed out of a crack in a quarry wall. I had a bunk for myself, one for my orderly, a little table on which I wrote, a small open fireplace, some shelves, and a couple of benches. I brought several candles with me, also some paper and a pen. I made ink by placing some lead from an indelible pencil in water. So as my boys would say, I was all "Jake," which meant O.K. We had a "galley," a kitchen was never called anything but a galley in the Marine Corps, which was fashioned just like my own abode; and so we lived like kings. The rest of the company was about a half or three quarters of a mile away. So I was commander there.

I was feeling fine and they said I was getting fat, but I didn't know as to that. During this time I first blossomed out with a mustache. We were brigaded with the French, and one of the officers made a few derisive comments about my youthfulness. He thought I looked more like a boy. By growing the mustache, I aged five years in the Frenchman's eyes. I became rather attached to it and have never bothered to shave it.

On April 23, when we were on the move, some of the officers had to hike 8 or 9 miles under heavy marching order. I got up the next morning at 4:30 , walked another 10 miles, and then that night I added 5 more with a 65 pound pack on my back. My men did not have to do all this though. We officers had a lot of reconnoitering on our hands. Around that time, I attempted to look up some of my hometown friends. In one of the *Intelligencers* I saw Bob Groves' address, and found that his battery was within a couple of miles of my camp. I walked to a few battery headquarters, but could not get his exact location before I had to move. I also looked for my friend Ben Morris, but didn't know where his outfit was.

In early May, BG. Charles A. Doyen, USMC, our 4th Brigade (Marine) commander, was relieved because of ill health and was replaced by BG James G. Harbord, USA. At first we were insulted at having an Army general in charge of a Brigade of Marines. When our unit moved back to Serans, France from the front lines, we were marched back under BG. Harbord's orders, to a large chateau with a big barn and were completely outfitted from head to toe with newly issued Army uniforms. And from that time forward we were served vegetables and fruit at our meals. We swore by the new general after that. He even put on Marine Corps Officer insignia. BG. Harbord wanted to get some action as a commander, so he was put in charge of our brigade. Later, after Belleau Woods, General John J. Pershing, Commander of the American Expeditionary Forces (AEF) gave him command of the 2nd Division, AEF. Following this division command, BG. Harbord was placed over all logistics within the American Expeditionary Forces. BG. John A. Lejeune, USMC, followed Harbord as brigade commander and was promoted to MG and became the new division commander after Soissons, when BG. Harbord left for the AEF "Service of Supply." MG. Lejeune, a graduate of the USNA but a Marine Corps General, so a Marine commanded our division from that point on.

So to recap my movements from my arrival in France through early May, we landed at St. Nazaire on February 5, 1918, stayed in port until the afternoon of the 8th, then boarded a train. We traveled east through Nancy and on into the Vosges where we detrained at a little hamlet called Damblain on Feb. 11. The next day we hiked over to our billets at Robecourt. All the Marines were gathered in that vicinity, in the two towns already mentioned, in Germanvilliers, Chaumont la ville, Blevaincourt, Vrecount, and others. There we stayed and trained until March 12, when our Regiment started for the front. We went through Senilly to Lemmes, detrained there and marched through, Aimsmont, Diene, and Sommedieu to a camp 2 miles beyond the last mentioned place. Then on March 25, we went to the front lines. Our company had its headquarters at Mont-sous-Les-Cotes and my platoon occupied Villers. There we stayed ten days, then went back to camp. After staying there 8 days, we went up for five days to Tresavaux and Eparges. My company occupied part of a large hill known as de Hures. Then we were suddenly drawn over to the Verdun sector and in late April we were supporting the front line behind Watsonville and Ronvaux.

Throughout those first three months, I had yet to see my first boche out of captivity. We got plenty of shells, but they were directed mainly at the artillery, and we had two casualties within the 78th company; Pvt. Raymond Crow, USMCR, killed on the afternoon of Friday, April 26 and another with a leg broken by a shell—also on April 26. They were both employed in the kitchen well back of the lines. None of my men has had so much of a finger scratched from fighting. One evening while at Villers we did witness a German raid on Handimont in which there were several French prisoners captured and some other casualties. But everywhere that I had been, the game had proved tame. Of course we had to be on our toes at all times, but if one took any unnecessary risks, there was little danger.

In early May, we moved up in front again, and my platoon was as usual in the front line. But things remained quiet. With the exception of a little scattered sniping, from which we were well protected, our company was still unmolested. We heard rumors at that time that we were to go up to the Somme front but we did not know for certain what the future held.

6

BELLEAU WOOD

We were relieved from duty in the Verdun Sector on the morning of Sunday, May 12, and during the last days of May, we were alerted that we would soon see some real action. General Pershing came up and looked us over, the first and only time I saw him. We had come back into a little town, and Pershing inspected us with Captain Messersmith. I remember his saying, "Very fit body of men, very fit body of men, Captain." Our fitness would indeed soon be tested.

On the evening of May 30 we were ordered to stand by in preparation for movement to the front lines. We anxiously awaited as darkness fell. At 10:00 p.m. no *camions* had yet arrived. *Camions* were the big French transport trucks which moved us up to the front. Each held about 30 men, and they were usually driven by French Indochinese. Finally at midnight we were told to get what sleep we could. The *camions* began arriving in the early morning hours of May 31st, and by 10:00 a.m., the entire division was en route to Chateau-Thierry.

We did not know it at the time, but our original orders were to relieve the Army's 1st Division, the "Big Red One," at Cantigny. We were to have used the French and British methods of trench warfare which had been developed during the first four years of the war. The French used "shock troops," young inexperienced troops, who would map out their objectives, rehearse what they were to do in order to gain a small parcel of land, and then attack with a tremendously high casualty rate. When these "shock troops" had suffered enough casualties to lose their efficiency, the old *poilus*, the veteran French troops with their curlicue mustaches, would relieve the young troops and dig in. A more horrid way of conducting warfare has not been invented. American forces were under French command at Cantigny, so Pershing's pet 1st Division had the honor of attacking, playing the role of the "shock troops," and we in the 2nd Division were to have played the part of the old *poilus*.

However at this same time, the end of May, the advancing Germans broke through near Chateau-Thierry and were closer to Paris, 75 miles, than at any time since the first months of the war. No tried French or British troops were available to send in. Our orders for Cantigny were cancelled, and we were sent the 75 miles to the Chateau-Thierry front. As we travelled to the line on the evening of May 31, we met people being evacuated from the front, farmers on their horse-drawn wagons with their household goods on top and cows hitched behind. We met two or three stray French soldiers, sampling their canteens of wine, eating cheese and crackers. They told us they were the last of their bloodied units. Although the French were glad to see us, they said on many occasions, "It's too late." We could see that no front line was left.

We arrived at our destination about noon of June 1 and were told to dig fox holes in what was a quiet open wheat field. Whenever I was up front before, we had deep dugouts for our protection against artillery fire. But here there was nothing but a few little holes in the ground which we dug with shovels about the size of spoons. The only map our battalion had was a little hashered map about six inches square and very inaccurate. Our company commander did not even have a map. The countryside looked perfectly placid, but late in the afternoon we saw the advance German forces coming into the edge of the woods, facing us across the beautiful wheat covered valley. We sat, staring at the enemy five hundred yards away, and awaited the order to advance.

Behind us in the clouds we could see four or five of our tethered captive observation balloons, and similar balloons on the German side. One of our planes flew over and put an incendiary bullet in one of the German balloons, and it fell to the ground in flames. This infuriated the Heinies, and they sent their planes over and knocked all ours down. That was the only air action I ever observed over there. We did hear reports of planes dropping handfuls of darts on the enemy. From the sky these would go right through a person if they struck him.

We had to wait for our artillery, which was longer to arrive since it all had to be moved by horse drawn wagons. Our galleys were also horse-drawn and did not appear for a few days. The mule which pulled our battalion's rolling kitchen made the supreme sacrifice during the trip. Our stranded mess sergeant, the resourceful Turner, stole a beautiful French saddle horse, threw mud all over him so as not to arouse suspicion, and rigged him to the galley, so our kitchen did arrive eventually. During the meantime our rations were limited, and a stray cow that appeared in the valley stirred great interest. As she wandered around, grazing between the lines, both sides tried to entice the cow to come to them. Eventually she wandered over to the woods across from us and disappeared. We were quite envious, envisioning the Germans drinking fresh milk or dining on beef.

We faced the German lines for five days, but exchanged only a little desultory sniping. The Lieutenant in charge of the platoon next to mine, 2ndLt. Henry L. Eddy, USAR, 82nd Co. (I), got his the second day, poor kid. He never regained consciousness. Finally, on Thursday, June 6 at 5:00 p.m., by which time our artillery was in place, our boys were given the command to advance. Our regiment was widely stretched out on the front line east of Belleau Woods. The 3rd Battalion, 5th Marine Regiment under Major Benjamin S. Berry, USMC, was to our left. Major Berton W. Sibley, USMC, Commanding Officer of the 3rd Battalion of our regiment, was ordered to pass through us for the advance, and our 2nd Battalion was ordered to hold the line. We watched in horror as the 1st Battalion from the 23rd U.S. Infantry Regiment on our right was given the command to advance. They went across the open field toward a woods occupied by the Germans. It was the most ghastly thing to watch as soldiers were just falling one by one out there. Advancing in extended order drill, they were sitting ducks for the German snipers and had no chance to cross the field.

We began exchanging sniper fire with the Germans in an open field overlooking the French village of Bouresches. By this time the enemy artillery had come up close behind the front lines, and for the first time we were exposed to accurate high explosive fire, which we referred to as the German "whizz-bangs." The fumes were so strong in the haze of the late afternoon that the men in my platoon called to me that they were being gassed. I got out of the foxhole and went along the line to calm my men first, and then reported what was happening to my company commander, Captain Messersmith, about 150 yards away. While passing through an area known as Triangle Farm on my way to the captain's Post of Command, I suddenly felt as if a baseball had hit me in the groin. I was knocked down and was very much surprised to see myself bleeding. I figured that I had been knocked down by some blunt shrapnel. I was able to struggle to my feet and continue about 80 to 100 yards to the Co. Post of Command and from the look on his face, I could tell that Captain Messersmith thought I was done for. He looked at my wound and was very solicitous. He had me lie down, called for a stretcher, and put me on it. Then he ordered the stretcher bearers to carry me back to a little French farm house nearby.

Capt. Messersmith was very fond of me, and I learned later that he wrote the citations that resulted in my receiving the Army Distinguished Service Cross and later the Navy Cross. Having been wounded at 7:30 p.m., I saw only about two and a half hours out of the more than three weeks of the Allied offensive at Belleau Wood. But I was there and made my small contribution to that famed fray. The attack we made was the first chance the Marines had to show what they really had, and I am mighty glad we got it. Of course we had to pay the cost, rather dearly too. But "*c'est la guerre.*" I later learned that on that day—June 6, 1918—the Marines suffered more casualties than on any day in their history up to that point.

7

MEDICAL CARE AND CONVALESCENSE

In the farm house I was placed on a sofa with my head on the lap of a wounded officer named Walton. He had been severely gassed, although I did not know it at the time. I think I was exposed to residual gas from his clothing, since I soon had a good deal of congestion in my breathing. The wounded were then loaded onto a truck full of straw covered beds. We made a brief stopover at Meaux where medics looked at us and then placed us on another truck bound for the large American Base Hospital #21 at Neuilly-sur-Seine, just outside of Paris. Since the action at Belleau Wood had not been foreseen, no arrangements had been made for the casualties. We arrived in the middle of the night. I was on an uncomfortable French stretcher which hit me in the calf of the legs and back of the neck. Most of the casualties there were from our outfit. I lay on the French stretcher in the corridor of the hospital for two days before being operated on. Before my operation, I was able to send a cablegram to my father, stating only "WOUNDED IMPROVING FEELING WELL." I also wrote by hand a short reassuring note to my mother, even though I did not yet know the nature or extent of my injury. My parents had already received the official telegram reproduced below. I have often wondered of the terrible uncertainty and pain that this must have caused them.

WESTERN UNION TELEGRAM
RECEIVED AT B -1 KS ED 61 GVT

DN WASHINGTON DC 18 14
MR SANFORD SELLERS LEX MO.
DEEPLY REGRET TO INFORM YOU CABLEGRAM
JUST RECD STATES YOUR
SON LIEUT JAMES MCBRIDE SELLERS MARINE
CORPS SEVERELY WOUNDED
IN ACTION JUNE SIXTH IMPOSSIBLE AT THIS TIME
TO ASCERTAIN FURTHER
PARTICULARS OR TO SEND INDIVIDUAL CABLE-
GRAM OF INQUIERY AS TO
CONDITION IF FURTHER REPORT IS RECD WILL
ADVISE YOU BY TELEGRAM
GEO BARNETT
MAJ GENL COMMANDANT
8351 15

I was really very lucky not to have gotten it worse than I did. Before I had been operated on, I really did not know anything about my wound. A machine gun bullet, not a piece of shrapnel as I first surmised, had struck me very low in the left groin, about two inches from the center of my body, and passed through my left buttock. The bullet did not lodge in me. The bullet made such a clean hole that I did not bleed very much, though. I was most fortunate because the bullet missed the bones and passed below my abdominal wall. If it had gone from the point of entrance to the exit in a straight line, it would have pierced the bone. So it must have curved around the pelvis. After two days I was operated on by a splendid surgeon. He opened up the passageway, and found that no bone had been touched. I remember coming out from under the ether anesthesia just as if I were drunk. After that I underwent treatment with an antiseptic known as the Dakin's fluid. A rubber tube perforated with small holes was placed in the open wound and by means of it the Dakin's liquid continually moistened the flesh. Very soon the wound healed in this way. The Dakin's solution was really nothing more than watered-down Clorox, but it was effective. I suffered only when the bandages were removed the first two times after the operation. Every morning the doctor dressed it anew, and I had no fever at all initially, my pulse was normal, and I felt most cheerful and lively under the conditions. And the luxury of real sheets and hot water baths made up for any inconveniences I may have suffered.

Owing to the crowded condition of our hospital, at first I was not in an officers' ward, but I was soon moved to one. Our ward, I was told, was one of the best in the hospital, very clean, pretty, well lighted, and ventilated. There were two French officers and three Americans besides myself; so we had a most congenial little group. A French Lieutenant was next to me. I learned some French from the him, and he in turn, learned a little English from me. His expression was "Smoking is bad for ze health." My French was *Del'eau c'est le meilleur boisson du monde*, which meant, "Water is the best drink in the world." I always made fun of him for drinking too much wine, while he gave me a hard time about my smoking habit. The French had the advantage over us because a great many of their lady friends could visit them daily, and our presence did not deter them from making the most affectionate of demonstrations. It was rather amusing when the parents of the French Lieutenant visited him, and one of his lady loves peeped in at the door. She retired instantly and would not enter until the old folks were gone. This happened several times.

The other Frenchman was a small handsome captain, with a winsome smile. He had a wife who was amazingly like a monkey in looks, but who was as amiable and kind as her husband. The two were absolutely devoted to each other. She brought him flowers, fruit and occasionally enough preserves to pass around to the rest of us. We had definitely established friendly relations with our allies.

The American boys in there with me those first weeks were: a Lieutenant Peterson from Minnesota who spoke English but with the trace of a Swedish pronunciation, and who suffered considerably from a fractured leg wound which had a tendency to hemorrhage; a Lieutenant Howes, an old Army Sergeant with a sense of humor and the appearance of a man of 25, but he had a son 18 years old in the Navy, and another 14 years old. He was operated on for appendicitis and the first time he went out, he won a bet from the nurse there by drinking 11 schooners of beer and returning on foot with no ill effects. The third officer was a Lieutenant Hays from Wisconsin, wounded in the shoulder by a bullet which broke his clavicle He got his in the same fight with me; so we had something to discuss. I was the only Marine there though. A good many wounded Marines came in to visit me however, and one of the nurses was the wife of a Marine Officer; so she looked after me pretty well and directed visitors up to see me. I got along elegantly and in fact I would have a good long rest.

One day a wheelchair was pushed in to my room containing 2ndLt. Tommy W. Goodwin, USAR, who was initiated into the Beta chapter at Chicago when I was. You might imagine my surprise. He was a US Army Reserve lieutenant and had been assigned to the 67th Co. (D), 5th Marine Regiment a few weeks before. A bullet tore a little gash in his left chest, only a flesh wound, but would have passed through his arm if he had not raised it a moment before.

Many American women served as aides in the hospital. One was a Mrs. Vanderbilt, a real Vanderbilt. An old Marine sergeant whom she had befriended asked what her name was. When she said, "Mrs. Vanderbilt," he immediately replied, "Glad to know you, I'm General Pershing!" A lot of humor helped alleviate the suffering. One young joker said that he arrived in France with 53 pieces of luggage—a fountain pen and a deck of cards!

We also frequently had entertainments. Elsie Janis, the famous chanteuse and actress, sung for us a couple of times, and I had a little chat with her one day. She was really doing her bit, and was very much loved by the A.E.F. Her mother trailed around with her all the time like a doting old hen. Elsie would come into a ward and without any accompaniment render us a good old American Rag, and if there were any French present she would give the translated version for them. I admired her very much; she sung so very much that most of the time her voice was rather husky, and the lack of accompaniment was rather trying. But she showed the pep.

By the first week of July, I began enjoying myself a good deal more, because I could get out of bed and mosey around. I had a fever for a while but it had all but disappeared, and there were a good many of my friends there with me. The Doctor continued to dress the wound every morning, and I considered all the surgeons to be wonders. The one who had me was in Germany when the war broke out. He attended the Heinies, later the Belgians, but was released from Germany and began caring for the French and Americans; he knew a great deal about gunshot wounds.

I had been moved in late June; so I then had a little room with one other American. We had a fine view of a pretty boulevard, and it was much quieter than in our former ward. The officer with me was an Engineer Lieutenant who was wounded during the same fight when I got mine. He had a huge hole in his back and a machine gun bullet glanced off a notebook in his left breast pocket making a small wound. But he was feeling as well as I.

There were some remarkable wounds treated there. Bullets were sometimes deflected in strange ways. I ran into a fellow who was in my fraternity in Chicago. He had been shot in the center of his chest and the bullet came out in the middle of his back, but it had hit a rib, circled around, and had emerged without penetrating his lung. Two fellows in the hospital with me were shot in their cheeks and the bullet came out in the back of their heads. The only difficulty one had was a diminished sense of smell, and the other was quite well except his mouth was wired shut. I could not understand how my bullet failed to hit any bones in my hip; I could only be thankful that there was a God who looked after us at all times. I made a number of new friends in the hospital; we got to know each other pretty well, among them a fine young Texan whose right leg the Doctor was fighting to save. He seemed to be growing stronger but was frightfully underweight. Even when everybody was laid up there was an awful lot of joking going on. I had never seen such a cheerful bunch as all the wounded Americans were. Every ward had its standard jokes and jokers. Naturally nearly everyone improved under these conditions.

The most cheerful officer in our bunch had both legs off above the knee & two fingers gone from one hand. He was married shortly before he sailed, and one day a letter came from his wife saying that she was sending him a pair of socks. He thought it was a great joke. All the doctors and nurses were simply crazy about him naturally. I often wondered what happened when he went back in that condition, having just been married.

In another case an officer had no wound at all but was in bad shape psychologically. He had been in a trench where heavy artillery rounds had fallen and buried him with a couple of others on top of him. The two above him died of suffocation. He felt that he too would die, but the index finger of his right hand was by his nose, and he could move it and get air to his nostril. He was buried several hours. He told me that he gave up several times and tried to end it all by holding his nostril closed, but just could not, and he was finally dug out. I do not know if he ever recovered from that experience or not. We all became so used to seeing suffering combined with cheerfulness that only the most remarkable instances made any impression on us. It was rather strange to note how much better the youngsters could stand the gaff. There were a couple of wounded Majors there who were the biggest babies you ever saw, although neither of them was seriously wounded.

The French had a big parade to honor the Americans on the Fourth of July. The Navy sent a limousine out to take four or five of us down to see the celebration in Paris. One platoon represented our battalion. It was led by 2ndLt. Clifton B. Cates, USMC, my best friend during the war and a graduate of Missouri Military Academy, one of Wentworth's big rivals. He later served as the 4th Marine Division's Commanding General during World War II and as Commandant of the Marine Corps during Harry Truman's administration. Clif was a character. When a German plane flew overhead, Clif would draw out his pistol and try to shoot the plane down. He had great amounts of charisma, and his men loved him. He was also quite a craps player. Back at Quantico he shot craps with Colonel Harry Lee's cowardly translator, Sgt. Sydney J. Colford Jr., the camp clown whose main job was to find liquor for the colonel. At the end of the evening, Colford gave Clif an I.O.U. for $3,000, which Clif tried to pawn off for three cents on the dollar. Of course, no one bought it. However, after the war Colford married a Vanderbilt divorcee, so the I.O.U. was good! I wish I had bought it from Clif when I had the chance.

In late July, an aide, Nina Nation, who attended the University of Chicago with my brother Ovid, stuck her head in my ward and informed me that I had a visitor. In walked Ovid in uniform. I was never more surprised and pleased in my life. I didn't know he was a commissioned chaplain, much less that the was on his way to France. Nor did I know that he had married his wife Katherine. He had been newly assigned to the 17th U.S. Field Artillery Regiment, a unit of my own division. The 2nd Division had three regiments of artillery—one heavy for the whole division, the 17th Field Artillery, and then the two light, 12th and the 15th Field Artillery. Ovid's instructor, Captain Houlihan, had recommended him for that assignment so that he could be near me. He learned from the service paper, *Stars and Stripes*, that I had been wounded and took a chance on finding me in the Neuilly hospital. With no mail for a month, I had thought he was still in Chicago, a young bachelor.

After fraternal greetings, my Scotch instinct broke out, and I asked him about the money orders I had mailed him, but he had not received my gambling winnings. Ovid gave me all the dope from home, fresh, because he had just landed the week before. I had thought that my brother Sandy was still in the States, and I found that he had been in France for several weeks. Sandy was Company Commander of a machine gun company in the Army's 89th Division. He was three years older than I was, and I really thought it a shame that he did not get a majority. Ovid stayed with me for two days, and we had a fine reunion.

Stars and Stripes gave us word of what was going on in the war and the world. The war correspondents often mentioned the Marines along with the Army and Navy, but our two regiments were the only two Marine Corps units involved in the war. The Army boys gave us a lot of static because of all the publicity we received. The 9th and 23rd U.S. Infantry Regiments did exactly the same things we did, but they never got any press, while we hogged headlines. Our 2nd Division and the 3rd Division were grave enemies. Our division was never actually in the town of Chateau-Thierry during that offensive, but the paper reported that we were. The 2nd Division was in the Chateau-Thierry front, but the 3rd Division had a Machine Gun Battalion (7th Machine Gun) which had actually been in the town. So this publicity about the Marines at Chateau-Thierry rubbed them the wrong way, and they let us know about it. However, one of their outfits, the 7th U.S. Infantry Regiment, came up to relieve one of ours in the Belleau Woods sector, and instead of advancing, they lost ground, and so our reply to them was, to their chagrin, "At least we didn't capture our own artillery!" Correspondents also occasionally reported our outfit in hand to hand combat, but I never saw any. With all our training firing rifles and pistols, it made no sense to stick a man with a bayonet when you had the option of shooting him.

In August, I was moved from Paris to Vichy, a regular little summer resort where I certainly enjoyed life. There were all sorts of medicinal springs there, which served as a drawing card for rich Parisians who were too fat, too thin, or thought there was something wrong with their health. So the town was very gay with their comings and goings. Our hospital faced the central park of the city, and since the doctors let me out, I could go out and mix with the maddening throng.

There were three or four movie shows in town, a symphony orchestra which was there permanently, and about once or twice a week we had a little Grand Opera. Among other operas, I attended "Le Jongleur de Notre Dame" and "Madame Butterfly." The singers were from various European Opera Companies, and I heard some splendid singing. It was a great life for the *blesse*. I would go out for a stroll in the park, a game of billiards, and the afternoon concert given by the orchestra. Then, in the evening, I would attend a vaudeville or movie show. In spite of the fact that everything seemed so nice there, I was getting tired of it all and wanted to be pushed back with my outfit. I had been inhabiting hospitals for such a long time that I felt out of touch with the boys up front, and I feared I would get fat and lazy from the loafing.

Most of the boys there made friends with French families, but I didn't have the inclination. I talked with a lot of French people, but it was rough sledding for me, and I didn't enjoy it much. It was very amusing to walk through the park and see a family of Frenchies trying to make conversation with an American Doughboy. There was much consultation of dictionaries.

Many gestures were in evidence, great good feeling prevailed, but very little comprehension.

It took quite a long time before I received any mail. When we were evacuated from the front line, no one knew where we would land and the tracking system was not too efficient. It was quite annoying to get wounded because the poor "*blesse*" lost all his baggage, personal belongings, and almost his identity, and the Postal Service seemed determined to cut him off from the outside world. But "*c'est la guerre.*" I arrived at the hospital with nothing of my own except a fountain pen and a pocketbook. Finally in mid-August I received mail, 40 letters, for the first time since middle May. It was certainly surprising to me to find out how many of my friends found out so soon that I was wounded and sent letters at once. I simply reveled in my mail and was the envy of my entire ward. But "hully gee" it was a long time coming.

My wound healed very rapidly through August, and late in that month I went before the disability board which classified the patients when dressings were no longer necessary for their wounds. My doctor assured me that I would go into class A, which meant that I was in excellent physical condition and fit for any service, and indeed I was rated class A. I knew it would not be long before I would be back with the boys again. I tried to keep up with my unit and knew that our division caught it so heavily in the recent drives that they were behind the lines reorganizing. I hoped that this work would be completed before I returned because it was very monotonous to have to drill, drill, drill all the time when we were in the back areas.

I first heard from my brother Sandy at about that time. I had thought that perhaps his division, the 89th, had gone up front during the recent drives. But up to the time he wrote they had not. A great many troops which had just arrived were sent to the front during the emergency. They had scarcely any training and lost heavily on that account. But it took much less time to train troops at that point than it did the pioneers. Things were becoming more systematized.

I was finally released from the hospital in Vichy about the first of September. Finding my way back to my company proved to be quite a trick. Having been away from my unit since June, I was completely out of touch with the paymaster and had no money whatever in my wallet. I wandered around awhile without knowing the location of my outfit, but finally hitched a ride with a Captain, Edwin Denby, USMCR, who was on detached duty from Marine Barracks, Washington D.C. I borrowed a hundred francs from him, which I told him I would probably never be able to repay. Denby would later become Secretary of the Navy in 1921.

We had to go through all sorts of replacement camps and depots, which required time. On my way back to the outfit, I had one shattering experience near the city of Blois. I had to eat meals somewhere, so I innocently joined an outfit for mess. A young lieutenant had lined up and was giving orders to a group of officers, some of them majors, which I found horribly odd. Not until I was in this formation to go to a meal did I learn what it was all about from another Marine who was on his way back too, and had been there a couple of days. He informed me that this was the place where they sent all the officers who had been accused of cowardice or shirking their duty. I had talked to some before I realized the situation, and they told some hair raising stories about how somebody had it in for them. I did not see any Marines except the one who like me was on his way back to his outfit. They were all Army, and I departed as soon as possible.

It took several weeks before I could rejoin the boys. At the time I didn't know to which organization I would be returned. Robert E. Messersmith, my former captain was by then a major and had a battalion of his own, the 2nd Battalion, 5th Marine Regiment. At least two wounded lieutenants originally in my company had been reassigned and sent behind the lines after being discharged from hospitals, because they had not yet fully recovered. But my wound, although it looked serious at first, healed up in fine shape, and I was as strong as ever.

In my wanderings I met 2ndLt William Wallace Ashurst, USMC, and we had a long chat. He had been hit in the arm and leg, but not at all seriously. However, a little piece of bone was nicked out of his arm, and he had to remain in the rear for a month or two until he regained complete use of the arm. He had received no mail at all since he was hit and didn't know anything about his people back home.

At that point in time, I thought that the worst fighting was over for the season. The war reports were certainly encouraging, and everything looked well for a favorable end to the whole affair. The most encouraging item outside of military affairs was the rise in the rate of exchange for French money. During August and September the franc changed from 5.70 francs = $1.00 to 5.45 francs = $1.00. The bankers said that this fact meant greatly increased confidence in the Allies by the neutral countries.

By the third week of September, I was still unsettled but rapidly approaching my destination. I caught up with the division the night of September 19 and with my regiment on September 21. But I still did not know which company I would join. While trying to catch my unit, I was able to hike 12 miles without any trouble at all. This was the first real exercise I had taken, and I was glad of the opportunity to test my strength; I truly found that I was as good as ever.

My outfit was back in the training area, and we expected to stay there for some time. They said that in the recent offensive, St. Mihiel there were hardly any casualties, except in my old battalion which ran into a machine gun nest. Otherwise it was simply a practice march. The Germans were already packed up and prepared to come over as prisoners, giving no resistance.

8

BLANC MONT

I finally found my battalion on September 22 at Domgermain, and I was reassigned to the 78th Company; I quickly discovered that I was the senior officer. As I said, Capt. Messersmith had been promoted to major, so I was in command of the company. I did not know for how long I would retain that position, as I was still a first lieutenant. Becoming a company commander was quite a jolt. Before my injury all the company commanders had been much older, and here I was, 23 years old and completely disengaged from my company for three and a half months, with command of my unit thrust upon me. But I did not have time to ruminate on the potential difficulties of my position. I had responsibilities—things to do and men to look out for, and I settled down quickly.

Major Holcomb had moved to the regimental staff, and we had a new battalion commander, Major Ernest C. "Bull" Williams, USMC, a simple kind of soul who liked to leave everything up to his adjutant while he tried to get up to the front line with an automatic rifle. While we were waiting for our next move, five regular captains were assigned to the battalion as replacements, but Williams would put nobody over Clif Cates, still a first lieutenant in command of the 96th

Company (H). He also left me in command of the 78th Company (E). One of my good friends from Quantico, 1stLt. Lucian H. Vandoren, USMC, had become battalion adjutant and really ran the battalion administratively, so I think he made the decision to leave Cates and me in command. I never knew what Williams had the excess five captains doing.

The 2nd Division, AEF, during my absence had seen action at Soissons in July and then at St. Mihiel in September, two of the bloodiest battles of the war. The company had received a great number of casualties while I was recuperating, and six times they had brought replacements up to fill the vacancies. I never knew some officers who served in my company. The men had a less strenuous engagement against the enemy at Pont-a-Mousson in early August. Pont-a-Mousson was what the French would refer to as a *"bon sector."* Very little fighting went on, so our men had free time to raid the nearby plum trees and to bathe in the river separating us from the Germans. Both sides used the river alternately with a sort of gentlemen's agreement not to bother each other.

On September 27, we got our orders to move out. Every time we moved up, we knew there was going to be a fight soon. If they gave us a ride in *camions* or if they sent around commendations from Pershing or some French commander, we knew our number was about to be called. Here is reproduced one of the many congratulations we received and which we hated so much to get:

> GENERAL GOURAUD, the distinguished Commander of the IVth French Army to which we are attached, has congratulated the Division on its wonderful success, and has reported to the COMMANDER-in-CHIEF of the French Forces that the German Army, east of RHEIMS, is in full retreat due to the magnificent attacks of the Division, and to its tenacity in holding its advanced positions.
>
> In transmitting this information, the Division Commander also desires to express to the officers and men of the Division his great

appreciation of their splendid performance, which demonstrates again their invincible fighting spirit and their superiority over the enemy soldier.

For a time, I thought I might be left behind. I had picked up a touch of bronchitis and was not feeling well. I went to the surgeon for treatment and he ordered me to rest in bed. I did not know that our unit was going into the line so soon or I would not have reported my illness to the Battalion Surgeon. Twenty percent of the men and one officer were always left behind; because of my condition I was the officer assigned to stay out. A captain had just arrived and had been assigned to the company, and for a while I didn't care much whether I went in or not. But the captain was assigned to another position just before we were to move out; I went to see the major and he had my orders changed and let me keep the company.

Before moving to the front lines, we would drop our 60-pound backpacks in the rear and put a guard on them, so our gear could be picked up later. We brought light combat packs up to the front, and these really consisted of no more than a mess kit, ammunition, and a poncho to ward off the elements. Each man was issued about 100 rounds with clips and belts. If someone ran out of ammunition, it was tremendously difficult to get more, but a man seldom fired all his rounds. While in the front lines we ate hardtack, bacon, and we were given bouillon cubes for soup. We considered ourselves particularly lucky when we got some canned food. I relish the memory of the one time I found a can of tomatoes, my favorite. They were delicious. Men would usually ration the water in the one canteen issued to them, and I cannot recall any instances of dehydration.

We learned that our division would again be under French command, having been specifically requested by their one-armed 4th French Army commander, General Henri J.E. Gouraud. We were to attack a rather sizable hill named Blanc

Mont Ridge, which dominated the surrounding area. The Germans had held it for four years and had proved too much for the French advance. We relieved the French units at midnight on Wednesday, October 2. We could see that sharp action had taken place there; my Company GySgt., Henry S. Brogan, and I sat on a hump in the trench the remainder of that first night only to discover with daybreak that two feet were sticking out from under the mound. We had been sitting all night on a dead Frenchman!

We were in trenches first occupied by the Germans and then by the French. These trenches were, of course, parallel to the front with traverses leading to the other parallel trenches behind and ahead. 2ndLt. Edward C. Fowler, USMCR, an old former South Boston policeman, and Pvt. Johnny J. Kelly, my orderly and one of my runners, came to me and said they would like to go forward and see what was in the next trench. After I okayed the mission, they explored the traverse and reached the next parallel trench to find it empty. The Germans, as was often customary, had been in these trenches at night and then had retreated to sleep in the rear during daylight. So my two Marines came back and reported that the next trench, which was a good deal better than the one we were in, was vacated. I sent a runner to the battalion commander and informed him of the situation, and he ordered the whole battalion to move up, which we promptly did.

This trench had some pretty nice dugouts. The one I was in had bunks and was joined to another room that was even larger. I put my five runners in the connecting room. We had no radio or wire communications at the company level. To get contact with the adjacent units, we sent out runners right and left. I could hear the runners talking that night. Pvt. Kelly was not backward, and he announced to the world that he was going to get the first machine gun the next morning. I keenly felt the adrenaline running through my system as he talked.

The next morning, Thursday, October 3, a runner came with

a field message stating that we were to attack at 5:55 a.m. I looked at my watch, and it was 6:00 a.m. Our artillery was very close behind us, and our light rolling barrage had started. I had a map showing the timing of the barrage by that time. I can still see myself slipping and sliding, climbing up the steps out of the dugout, and preparing our move forward. I immediately sent runners to each of the platoons, and we all started together.

Our battalion was the first wave. I might explain that when a division attacked, only two of the twelve battalions were in the front line. Each of the front battalions was backed up by five battalions in column. Our artillery had been brought up very close behind us, and the barrage they put down for our attack was so accurate that we could advance to within about fifty yards of the shell bursts. The Germans had set up their machine gun nests all over the hill so that the cross fire would cover the entire area. But with our very precise barrage, our men would be on top of the machine gun emplacements before the Germans could come up for air. Despite this advantage, our casualties were quite heavy.

After we went over the top and got out of the traverses, we were in open country, following the barrage. Before us, all up the hill, were German dugouts with machine gun emplacements manned by eight or ten men each. At 6:20 a.m. Pvt. Kelly ran out ahead as soon as he spotted a boche machine gun sputtering away at us, disappearing in the smoke of our own barrage. The barrage was not impenetrable; with luck one could get through it without being hit. Kelly charged up to a machine gun emplacement holding about ten Germans. He put the gunner out of action with a grenade. Another squarehead came out, and Johnny shot him through the heart with his pistol, which runners were entitled to carry. I was amazed that he hit the German, because our .45 Colts were difficult to shoot very accurately even under ideal conditions. The remaining eight Germans surrendered, and Pvt. Kelly proudly marched them back, waving to the boys and shouting, "I told you I was going to get the first one!" For his actions that morning, he was awarded the Medal of Honor both Army and Navy.

At 7:30 a.m., shortly after Pvt. Kelly's heroics, another member of the 78 Company, a stout young Marine named Cpl. John H. Pruitt, was also awarded a Medal of Honor both Army and Navy. When volunteers were called for, he went forward with three other Marines and charged right into a machine gun which was going full blast, and shot the gunman right between the eyes. Cpl. Pruitt single-handedly attacked and captured two German machine guns and crews. He killed two boches with his rifle during the fight; and then later he and a pal took 42 prisoners including 3 officers. Cpl. John H. Pruitt was KIA the following day, October 4th, while on top of the Massif. Later, in WW2, the U.S. Navy named a destroyer in his honor. I was very fond of both Cpl. Pruitt and Pvt. Kelly. Kelly was my orderly. Both were small Irishmen, appearing to be no more than seventeen; they looked just alike and were really pretty. They were two of only seven U.S. Marines to be awarded the military's highest honor in World War I.

These were merely a couple of instances which happened to come to my attention. The same sort of thing was going on up and down the line. The surprising part of it was that we did not have more casualties than we did. The French and evidently the boches couldn't understand the American methods of attack. The French advanced very carefully and cautiously and lost many more men than we did, because the squareheads (Germans) knew what to expect. We started over in a pretty formation but the fight soon degenerated into a sort of free for all, every man for himself and everybody right up behind the line of the barrage, which was proper. Heinie would go down into his dugout, and as soon as the barrage passed him our men were right there, and he didn't have a chance to come out and pepper us with his many machine guns.

The heroism of Pvt. Kelly and Cpl. Pruitt was not isolated. Time after time the courage of our men shone through. These men were trained and disciplined for any circumstances. When the fighting was thick and communications broke down, they had the intelligence and the intestinal fortitude to act on their own and continue to our objective, not needing their officers behind them, goading them on. They were Marines, and I considered them to be among the finest men the country had to offer. My proudest moment in France occurred that Thursday morning of October 3rd, 1918, at Blanc Mont Ridge, where I had the privilege of leading these men of the 78th Company over the top.

Our unit had received a number of replacements after the engagement at St. Mihiel in mid-September, which our boys had participated in just before I had returned to the company. A couple of these inexperienced young men were with me at one point during the fighting on Blanc Mont Ridge. We were going up a hill when a rabbit jumped up. About three or four of us were nearby, and although we were following our barrage, we all took a shot at it. A young boy right near me, a replacement, said, "This is kind of fun." The atmosphere was unreal. We were absorbing heavy casualties. I lost two of my best lieutenants during that advance, 2ndLt. Hugh P. Kidder, USMCR, and 2ndLt. John McHenry Jr., USMCR. One was about ten feet away from me when he was hit, and there was nothing I could do for him. I was pretty much broken up by their deaths; they were as fine a pair of boys as I ever knew. Another lieutenant was wounded so three of the six officers in my company were casualties. It seemed that we always had heavier percentage of losses among the officers than among the men. But we continued up and captured the hill. Strangely enough, I never remember encountering concertina or barbed wire in this or any other attack, although we sometimes laid some ourselves.

1stLt. Clifton B. Cates was on my company's left with the 96th Company, and the 80th Company was supposed to be on my right. I sent a runner to the 80th Company, but he came back and reported that he had reached the 79th Company, way to our right. The 80th Company was absent. It was commanded by a man named Capt. Walter A. Powers, USMC, and his first sergeant, GySgt. James Foley Jr., was a cashiered British officer. Powers never called a meeting with his platoon leaders to tell them what their assignments were. The company commander apparently wanted to save his skin and thought it would be dangerous in the front line, so he simply left his company. Some 80th Company men were aware later that an advance had begun. In small groups they tried to catch up, but we did not cover the front as we were supposed to. In spite of Powers' negligence, we got to our objective—a road parallel to our front —and dug in just on the other side of it.

At Blanc Mont Ridge we made the attack exactly the way we were trained to do. The regiment advanced six deep. Our battalion was the assault battalion, the 1st Battalion was behind us, the 3rd Battalion was behind them, and the three battalions of the 5th Marine Regiment followed our regiment, also in columns. We reached the summit of the hill, but Clif Cates' 96th Company on the left flank got considerable fire. The French divisions on either side of us had failed to keep up with us so our division had both flanks exposed for a time. Clif rearranged his company and faced the left flank. Three days later, when this situation had been ironed out, the 3rd Battalion came through us and attacked to the left, which was still occupied by the Germans. On our right the 9th U.S. Infantry Regiment advanced, followed by the 23rd. They apparently went over properly and did not have too much trouble.

When we got up to our final objective, Major Williams called for a conference of his company commanders. All of us went to his command post, including Capt. Powers, who had reached the front by that time. He and his first sergeant were by themselves. Capt. Powers, an impressive looking older fellow and a lawyer, came up and had a lot to say. But so much confusion abounded in the battle that none of us had yet realized what had happened. When we were relieved and going back on the line in column of squads, Williams checked on the 80th Company, and neither Capt. Powers nor GySgt. Foley Jr. were present. Williams began inquiring and found out the whole sordid story. Capt. Powers should have been court-martialed, but Williams was not much for paperwork. So he simply relieved Capt. Powers and put somebody else in command of the 80th Company. It seems almost unbelievable that in the confusion of the attack when we were widely scattered, his cowardice and complete lack of leadership were not discovered until several days later.

At Blanc Mont Ridge was the only time I ever saw a tank in action. A French tank appeared from nowhere on the road and came down our front. This happened when the 96th Company was facing the flank, and I am sure the French crew thought they were moving perpendicular to the front. When the tank reached our flank (the occupants did not know what they were doing anyhow), it came under fire immediately, and the Frenchmen conveniently ran out of fuel and abandoned their tank.

Two or three days later while we were still on the front line, 2nd Division Headquarters gave us the order to advance. The artillery had not come up, and we did not get very far. The order was ridiculous, shooting at the Germans with no artillery preparation. At that time my old company commander, Major Robert E. Messersmith, USMC, was in command of the 2nd Battalion, 5th Marine Regiment. He sent messages back to 2nd Division Headquarters that high casualties were being incurred and that this lunatic action had no chance of gaining ground. Finally, we were ordered to halt and dig in, and then later to draw back.

A young Marine captain named George W. Hamilton, USMC, was in command of the 1st Battalion, 5th Marine Regiment. He had a good reputation within the 5th and the 6th Marine Regiment and sent back word to 2nd Division Headquarters that he found Maj. Messersmith's battalion in full retreat, led by their major. Basing their actions on this report, they relieved Messersmith of his command. A little later I talked to Messersmith, a good friend. He asked for a hearing but never got one, because from then on until the armistice we were continually moving. The poor fellow was in a motorcycle sidecar with a corporal driving him and no command or responsibilities. He had looked after his men, and the messages he sent back were correct, since this later advance was ridiculous. I know. I advanced there.

The next day after this fruitless advance, we received orders to return to the lines which had been our original objective. The 142nd U.S. Infantry Regiment of the 71st Brigade of the 36th Division, AEF, not yet blooded, was ordered to join us. They came up and their troops moved right into the trenches with us. Our battle-weary Marines scared them to death with the gory tales of our experiences. When the order came for the 71st Brigade of the 36th Division to advance, their lieutenant colonel, a West Pointer, had a very difficult time trying to rout these inexperienced men out of their trenches and dugouts.

While advancing, we approached a huge German dugout, and I saw a couple of Germans going down into one of its two entrances. The procedure we followed in this situation was to approach the entrance and yell, *"Raus mitten"* [Come out]. If they came up, we took them prisoner, and if not, we threw a grenade down and continued on, leaving the dugout for the outfits coming behind to clean up. This particular dugout was right in my path, so I went through this procedure. No one came out, so I dropped a grenade and continued on ahead. Only 40 or 50 yards beyond that was our objective, a road, where we dug in. My runner at that time was just a young kid. In fact, my first sergeant had advised me to get a more conscientious one, the kind who would like to shine my shoes. Nevertheless, I retained him as my orderly. That evening he and a friend asked if they could go back to this dugout. Night was coming on and the weather was chilly. We did not carry cold weather gear in our combat packs, and they thought they might find some blankets in the dugout. I allowed them to return to the dugout, and they got halfway down when, much to their surprise, they heard this guttural German talking. They scrambled back up to the top and yelled, *"Raus mitten."* The artillery had been silent for a while, and Germans started coming up, one at a time, until, all told, 42 of them came out of the dugout. The boys lined them up and relieved each prisoner of his weapon. In addition they accumulated a whole pile of souvenirs—binoculars, pistols, pouches, and other personal gear.

One of my men, a real character, GySgt. Henry S. Bogan from Frankfort, Kentucky had received a *"bonne blesse,"* a good wound, a flesh wound in the arm. So, Bogan took all these 42 Germans and marched them back as prisoners. Later after the war, I had to give a speech on Blanc Mont Ridge, and Fort Leavenworth, Kansas, sent me a monograph from the German side on this particular action. The Germans had said: "Thus at one point there were [captured] 42 soldiers composed of several different branches. Some of them were Signal Corps, some were artillerymen, some were infantry. All were taken prisoner in one action."

This huge dugout was a much safer place than our trench near the road, so I went back and set up my command post in a space which could have housed a few hundred men. It had two entrances and was concrete lined with electric lights, run by a broken down generator housed in a small, separate building. Incidentally, that place was where I first got cooties (lice). The boche blankets were filled with cooties. Insects always did bite me. My wrists and arms were all chewed up. But we got used to all that, and it just made us better able to appreciate good surroundings when we got them.

While I was in this dugout and after we had established our lines, I sent a corporal to find Ovid, and he came up to see me at once. So then we sat in a former boche dugout and swapped stories. Of course his couldn't match mine because his outfit was usually "seven miles behind," and the casualties of his entire regiment couldn't equal those of any one of my platoons. Ovid said that during the recent battle, he had questioned all the wounded Marines he saw returning to the rear. As was always the case, their reports were totally dismal, and he said that he worried so much that a dream came to him of my being brought up for his professional services on the burial party. Wasn't that a fine thing to tell me?

The battalion surgeon, Ovid, and I were engaged in a conversation when a runner came up with the mail. One letter was addressed to Ovid, and I recognized it immediately. It was the postal money orders I had won playing craps! It had been returned to me since my brother obviously was no longer in Chicago, and my return address was on the letter. I had mailed it on St. Patrick's Day in March, and after a trip halfway across the world and back, it returned to me in October; the Scotsman in me was much relieved.

One U.S. Navy Medical Surgeon was assigned to each battalion, and he was kept plenty busy after one of our engagements. We had a staff of six Navy Corpsmen who assisted him in his duties. In the field, each company assigned a few men as stretcher bearers, and they knew enough rudimentary first aid to get casualties back to where the makeshift hospital was set up. Our battalion surgeon, whom I often saw in St. Louis after the war, had set up his facilities in my dugout, and casualties were brought to him down there. Some were suffering from shell shock and one of the symptoms of that was a frequent recurring spasm. The battalion surgeon would seat the soldier and hold his hand. He later asked me if I knew what he was doing, which I did not. He explained, "If you purposely try to grasp his hand firmly for any length of time, after about five minutes he will get so weak he has to stop, but if you have a genuine shell shock victim, the firm pressure just continues." I think 10 or 15 had genuine cases of shell shock. Everyone was a 36th Division man, not a single Marine. If a unit had a cadre, a nucleus of men who had been blooded, they could absorb a whole lot of replacements, and the newcomers would survive their first combat with no trouble. But the 36th was a completely new outfit, so they had a number of these shell shock cases.

On Thursday, October 10, we were finally relieved and started moving back to a rear area. We got only a mile or so when we were stopped and, to our great disappointment, made to give up all the new beautiful M1918 Browning automatic rifles, trench knives, and other new supplies which our Marines had liberated from the newly equipped 36th Division. On Friday morning, October 11, I learned that I had been promoted to a temporary captaincy, so I was then pretty sure of keeping my company. I rested easier since a good many Captains did not have companies, and I, while still a lieutenant, always thought that there was a chance one would be reassigned to the 78th. So I could then sport two bars on my shoulder. And when I got the chance, I increased my allotment to Dad.

After Blanc Mont Ridge, only 83 men were left in my company out of 250. There were just two men in my company who had been there since the beginning. All the others had been to the hospital with wounds or were new replacements. I had seen enough of the war to appreciate a little rest by then. Back in the States, a Canadian officer who was our instructor, said that any outfit that went over the top twice a year was more than doing its share. Well we had hit it once a month regularly since June. We were all beginning to wish they'd divide up the work a wee bit and give the boys just over from the States a chance. They were all so anxious to have a fight. But our boys had the stuff and whenever the High Command saw a hard nut to crack, in went our division and we never failed. I had the fightingest outfit you ever saw and I would have attacked the hottest spot in Old Nick's realm with them. We wouldn't have made a very pretty sight marching up Fifth

Avenue, because we were frayed at the knees, equipped partly with American equipment, partly with French, and nearly everyone had some boche stuff. I had a bedding roll, a map case, and a pair of binoculars which I copped from a Heinie officer. And the company carried around a couple of boche machine guns, so we could use the ammunition we captured. It was the funniest aggregation you ever saw when we got on the move; as someone said, we looked like the Swiss navy on parade. But we got there just the same.

Taken all together, Blanc Mont Ridge was the most skillful operation in which we participated, despite Capt. Powers' unforgivable actions as a Company Commander. My company did some marvelous work; we took more prisoners and machine guns than any other company. It was one of the proudest days of my life when we advanced, overcame all resistance, sent a long line of prisoners to the rear, and arrived at our objective exactly on scheduled time. That objective was one of the strong points of the far famed Hindenburg line. We received a great many glowing tributes, and even General Foch mentioned our drive. While we were still in the front line, French General Gouraud, our Army commander, issued a communiqué praising the 2nd Division, AEF, and reprimanding the French units on either side for not keeping up with us.

In addition, the whole 2nd Division, AEF, was cited three times in orders of the French Army for their gallantry, authorizing every member to wear the French *fourragere* (World War I). To the present day, every member of the 6th Marine Regiment wears the *fourragere*, a green and red citation cord, on his shoulder. General Gouraud also ordered 500 *Croix de Guerres* to be awarded to the 2nd Division, AEF. These were to be parceled out to the companies, and I was ordered to recommend sixteen men. I was easily able to do so, since we were in the attacking wave, and the men had plenty opportunity to distinguish themselves. As a result of my recommendations, the two Medal of Honors and eight Distinguished Service Crosses were also issued to the 78th Company. I believe all the company commanders, except Powers, received *Croix de Guerres*, which is where mine came from. I do not know who wrote the citation to back mine up, but it resulted in my also receiving the Silver Star Medal. I did not mind. I thought I rated a little something since I had done my part.

Our people went all out to get recognition when there was justification, and even sometimes when there was not. Sgt. Sydney J. Colford, was the translator for Lieutenant Colonel Harry Lee, who had assumed temporary command of the 6th Regiment after Colonel Albertus W. Catlin was wounded on June 6 at Belleau Woods. Colford was a notorious coward and did not make any bones about it. Word got around that he had received a *Croix de Guerre* at Blanc Mont Ridge, and everyone wondered what Colford possibly could have done to warrant a medal for bravery. The whole 2nd Division was laughing when we found that his citation read "For observing the attack of the 2nd Battalion, 6th Marine Regiment."

After Blanc Mont Ridge, we did a lot of moving back and forth, and marched the weary veterans and eager replacements up hill and down dale. Most of the time we were sleeping outside, and the weather was horrible. One night, I was over-joyed to find a sort of hut with a bed in it, but no sooner had I settled down than orders came to move again, and we moved about a couple of miles. When I finally was able to get some rest that night, I was lying down on my poncho with my First Sergeant and we did not know whether to put the poncho on top or underneath; we did not know which was wetter. Around that time, we did have a pleasant diversion when we were billeted in the small town of LaVerne north of Chalons near a hospital. We had a couple of dinner parties and a dance for some fine nurses. It was certainly a treat for us. We had just returned tired out from the front and had a chance to clean up, and step out into society.

9

THE MEUSE-ARGONNE

On Wednesday, October 20, we received orders to move to the Argonne Forest, where a battle had been raging since late September. By that time, General Pershing had finally won his argument with the High Command for an American front, so this battle was purely an American operation. We were encamped near Sedan. On Saturday, October 26, we got a visit from Major General Charles P. Summerall, USA, Commanding General, 5th U.S. Corps, and later superintendent of the Citadel. He was an extremely intelligent man. He put a huge map on the side of a barn and had our whole battalion assemble and sit down so he could talk to us. He showed us Marines where we were going to attack and explained exactly what the purpose of the offensive was. He said that if we captured our objective, we would cut off the whole German Army between there and the coast, and that ours was a place of honor in the impending American drive since we had already qualified as the "shock troops" of the American army. Then he spoiled it all by saying that if we did not do our jobs well, heads would roll. We considered that an insult to our outfit!

We relieved the great 42nd Division, AEF, which had gotten almost as much publicity as the Marines. It had a brigade commanded by BG. Douglas MacArthur, USA and was known as the "Rainbow Division", being made up of troops from all over the country. The 42nd was a National Guard Division as were all divisions numbered from 26 to 50. The divisions numbering from 1 to 25 were Regular Army and from 75 up were National Army divisions. My brother Sandy, for instance, was a machine gun company commander in the 89th Division, AEF, which was composed of draftees.

On Thursday, October 31, we received the following hand-written operation order to begin our advance the next day.

Headquarters
*   *2nd Bn, 6th Marines.*
*   *October 31, 1918.*
*   *Bn Order Secret*

This Regiment, in column of Bns., will attack on Day "D" at "H" hour. The Bns. from head to rear—1st, 3rd and 2nd. The 1st Bn. will take the 1st objective, where it will halt, and, upon a passage of its lines by the 3rd and 2nd Bns., will follow as reserve. The 3rd Bn. will take the 2nd objective; this Bn. will pass thru the 3rd Bn. at "H" + 650 hours and take the 3rd objective, and exploit toward exploitation line. Objectives and sector limits as marked on maps furnished.

This Bn. will follow the 3rd Bn. at a distance of 1,000 metres with two companies in the front line and two companies in the 2nd line. The 2nd line will follow the 1st at a distance of 500 metres. Order of companies from left to right, front line, 80th and 78th; rear line 96th and 79th. During the advance to the 2nd objective companies will proceed in 2 lines, with 2 platoons in each line, adopting such formations as the terrain and fire encountered make necessary, at all times keeping in such formation as will permit the Bn. to pass through the 3rd Bn. and continue the attack. After passing 2nd objective, companies will advance in wave formation on open ground, and by line of combat groups in woods. Upon arriving at 3rd objective, the position will be immediately organized in depth, companies retaining approximate positions

*maintained during the advance. Front line companies will send out
combat patrols to the front for reconnaissance and to seize and organize
commanding ground. Company positions will be organized in a series of
strong points.*

*The 5th Regt. will advance on our right, and a mixed Bn. will form
combat liaison with the 80th Division on the left.*

*Stokes Mortars and one-pounders will follow in rear of the 80th
Company. One machine-gun platoon will be with each support company,
and one platoon with Bn. Hqs.*

*Bn. P.C. will be in the successive P.C.'s of the 3rd Bn. and, after the
2nd objective, between the 2 support companies.*

By order of Major Williams

Lt. H. Vandoren

1st Lt. U.S.M.C.

Bn. Adjt.

That night, our artillery was brought up very close to us. It
was the only time I ever felt nervous. The artillery was just a
few yards behind us, firing all night, and I could not sleep very
well. I did not relish the situation and really felt uneasy. On the
morning of Friday, November 1, we began the attack in an
unusually long advance in leapfrog fashion. The 1st Battalion,
6th Marine Regiment, went over the top in the first wave, the
3rd Battalion, 6th Marine Regiment, passed through them, and
then we, in turn, passed through them to the front. When we
passed through the 3rd Battalion, the 78th Co. was on the left
flank. I had experience in map reading, but I got completely off
the track because our map did not show the declination, only
true north. So true North on our maps was actually to the East
of our line of advance. We veered way over to the north, my
left, toward an open field. We finally came to a drop off, and a
town which was not supposed to be there was below us. We
could see fighting between our forces and the Germans going
on around the town. I halted and passed the word of the error
over to Maj. Williams and we executed a right flank and moved

over to where we were supposed to be. But before we left, one of the replacement captains, Capt. Kirt Green, USMC, commanding the 80th Company, called his Platoon Commanders over to him for a conference. The Germans spotted the group and directed some small 37 mm cannon firing on the position and wiped out all the officers of the 80th Company. One of these young officers was a good friend, a very handsome fellow, 2ndLt. John G. "Jack" Schneider, USMC, from St. Joseph, Missouri and a graduate of Culver Military Academy. He was only wounded at that time, but while on his way to the rear for treatment, he was killed by intermittent firing.

We advanced about 11 or 12 kilometers the first day. That night, in the darkness, along came a regiment from the 9th or the 23rd U.S. Infantry Regiment, moving in column of squads up the main road going toward the front. They halted when they came to our line, so Maj. Williams and I went over and asked what was going on. Their regimental commander said, "I have orders to advance in column of squads. What about it?" Williams said, "Well it's as good a way to commit suicide as any I know of." But evidently our intelligence knew what was going on because they went on in column of squads all night and encountered no difficulty. We, however, did not proceed in column of squads; we advanced in regular extended order.

The next day we advanced and had practically no casualties. We picked up a few German stragglers during the march and encountered no difficulty. We also found many uncrated German weapons left by the roadside. The day was marked by one of the strangest moments of our months in France. A Y.M.C.A. man, riding in a motorcycle sidecar, traveled up a road looking for a suitable site for his headquarters. The Y.M.C.A. was found everywhere on the Western Front, providing assistance and entertainment for the men. He found a house which he thought would be a good place to set up shop. When he got there, he discovered the home was occupied by the headquarters group of a German regiment. They all surrendered to him!

A day or two later, as we continued our unabated advance, we entered a town with a church still intact. I went into the church and to my great surprise, found my brother Ovid. I always seemed to run into him in the most unexpected places. He had fixed the organ in the church and was playing it. We enjoyed the music and had a nice visit.

Although we were advancing easily, we were not allowed to attack and capture the venerable city of Sedan. Pershing had reserved that honor for the 1st Division, AEF, his "pride and joy." By Sunday, November 10, 1918, we reached the Meuse River. At 8:00 p.m., our outfit received orders from Headquarters, 2nd Division, AEF to hike ten kilometers to Mouzon and cross a bridge there at 8:30 p.m. that night. Of course that was an impossibility, and by the time we reached the crossing place, the barrage had stopped and the bridge had been blown up. The 5th Marine Regiment did cross at Villmontry, however, as well as parts of the 2nd Battalion, 354th U.S. Infantry Regiment 89th Division. Both units lost many men that last night of the war. During this entire advance we were hit by only nine casualties and no deaths.

I, however, was not with my men on the night of Sunday, November 10. One of my lieutenants, 2ndLt. Edward C. Fowler, USMC, and I had been compelled to drop out on account of the bowel trouble which was prevalent in the Division. We were tagged for a hospital, but just went to a vacant home where we could keep warm and quiet for a few days.

10

THE ARMISTICE AND OCCUPATION

At the eleventh hour of the eleventh day of the eleventh month, 1918, the armistice was signed. Soon after the announcement, General Summerall went to his men of the 5th U.S. Corps to congratulate them for keeping pressure on the German left flank in an attack, resulting in high casualties, they had made the night before. They gathered around him and he gave his speech, but the men gave him no applause or cheering. They just turned around and left, rather sullen with the fact that he had ordered the attack the night before. He was referred to as "General Kill 'em all" by the men after that. In fairness, however, I think Pershing had told him to keep the pressure on, and he probably should not have been faulted.

The news of the armistice came as a surprise and was obviously a great relief. Not having a roof overhead for two weeks combined with the cold damp weather was taking away our pep, and a great many of us had begun to feel a little under the weather. I was glad that sickness didn't get me till all the scrapping was nearly over. I stopped to see Ovid with the 17th U.S. Field Artillery Regiment, on the way to rejoin my company a day or two after the armistice. Ovid, as well as a number of the Marine officers, seemed inordinately glad to see me. Apparently the report of my death had been spread pretty widely. I spent the afternoon of Wednesday, November 13 reading Ovid's newspapers from home and the wonderful letters my mother had written to him, giving local news and news of Wentworth. We also had a good visit with Bob Groves, our fellow Lexingtonian and Wentworth alum. That night I slept with Ovid in his good French bed. He slept in his bag, and I quite comfortably rolled up in his blankets. The next morning we rode over to Sandy's outfit, just to our right. When we got there we met Duvall, who was a lieutenant in Sandy's battalion, and he told us that Sandy was away at a school. While we were sorry to miss Sandy, we were glad to know that all three of us came through the war whole. Realizing that our parents would be quite interested in whether we got through now that the armistice had been signed, Ovid arranged to send home a cablegram to our folks stating that we were all right, which was considerable relief to them.

I tried to get back to my company that afternoon, but succeeded only in getting rid of my kit, which went somewhere on my ration cart. I had found 2ndLt. Charles A. Ingram, USMCR, of my company also trying to get back. Ingram was in the twenty percent kept out of the battle. The ration cart was to pick us up and guide us out, but it slipped away without our seeing it, with my kit in tow. So we both stayed with Ovid that night. Colonel Robert H. Dunlop, USMC, who came to Ovid's unit from the Marines, invited the three of us to supper, and we had a fine beefsteak.

On Friday, November 15, 2ndLt. Ingram and I returned to our unit and found that the armistice had removed all concerns. 1stLt. Clifton Cates, I, and our men boldly lit fires, which we had previously not been able to do during the daytime since the smoke would give away our position to the Germans. We peeled off our undershirts and "read our underwear" for cooties. I counted over 30 about the size of a flea, and we all sat around crushing them between our nails.

A few weeks after the Armistice I sent the following letter home describing my activities and movements during the last two months of the war:

Nov 30 1918

    78th Co. 6th U.S. Marines

    Dear Mother,

    Now that the armistice is all signed up, and the authorities have loosened up on the censorship, I want you and Dad to grab out a big map, and I'll lead you around on our last two months trips.

    When I rejoined the Company, I found the boys billeted in a small village near Toul named Domgermain. The division had been billeted there as a reward for its excellent work, but we were warned to remain in readiness instantly to entrain and go again into the scenes of activity. So sure enough, after a week of comparative rest orders came, we boarded a train bound for destinations unknown and detrained at a small station south of Chalons named Vitry-la-ville and from there marched over to Serry or Sarry. Again we rested for two days (this was the last of September), and then we boarded camions, a sure sign that we were going into an attack. I thought for a while that I was going to be left behind, because I was feeling rather rocky at the time from a little touch of bronchitis, and the surgeon had me laid up in bed. At the time I didn't know that the Regiment was going into the line so soon or I shouldn't have turned in. There are always left behind 20 % of the men and an officer, and on account of my indisposition I was assigned to stay out. A Captain just arrived had been assigned to the company, and for a while I didn't care much whether I went in or not. But a couple of hours before we shoved off, the Captain was given another job, and I went around to the Major who, like a good sport, had the orders changed and let me keep the company. So away we went and got off just a little South of Souain, just North of Suippes. There we lived in some old trenches for a couple of days, awaiting the French, who had been attacking for a week and had run into some snag, the same being a stronghold known as Blanc Mont, just northwest of Somme-py, part of the Hindenberg line. The night we

112

relieved and the next morning I saw the most gruesome sights it is possible to imagine, for there had been a great deal of hand to hand fighting of the fiercest kind, much use of hand grenades and machine guns. That night the boches were firing their "typewriters" from nests not over 50 yards from our trenches, and they were so close that their flares were hitting in our own lines. The French are willing to allow them to stay that close, but our troops never do; but we were unable to do anything that night because we didn't know the ground. So there we lay out in the open trying to keep our feet from freezing and ducking machine gun bullets all the time. The next morning though, the Heinies retired to other trenches, evidently thinking that we couldn't advance, and planning to return to their strong points the next night. We stole a march on them, though, and I sent a platoon out to see what was going on. They took possession of the next line of trenches without exposing themselves, and along toward evening when two boche officers came strolling unconcernedly down the trench my outposts picked them up. We stayed in this advanced trench that night, but the next morning at 6:00 over we went behind the prettiest barrage that I've ever seen. This barrage made such a distinct line in front of us that it was possible for us to get within 50 yards of it. You know that the closer attacking troops are to their barrage the less chance there is for the enemy to get his machine guns started. So we surprised Heinie from the start and trapped dozens of them before they could get out of their dugouts. It was after this attack that Ovid and I wrote a note to Dad, so I won't describe it any more for fear of repeating myself.

We remained at our objective for about ten or twelve days when relief came, and back we went to a small town North of Chalons called La Verne. Here was where we met the nurses and had a little dance and dinner party. But we didn't rest long for after three or four days orders came to pack up, and we started out on the longest, hardest hike I've ever had. We marched to Suippes the first day, about 15 miles, and the next day we went to Leffincourt due north, near Machault, a distance of 25 miles, over trails slimy with mud and up and down hill. It turned out, however, that the French didn't need us for an expected emergency though, and back we hiked, only to find the dreaded camions again *awaiting us. This time we rode from near Suippes over through St. Menehould to Les Islettes, then hiked up to a field just south of Exermont. Two days later we attacked at Sommerance. This first day we advanced through Landres et St. George, Bayonville and stopped just south of Fosse. Two days later we pushed on through Fosse, Sommauthe and up to the left of Beaumont. We were still fighting when the armistice was signed, and it was at Beaumont that Ovid and I again wrote a combination letter to you. After the agreed delay we have taken up the march to the Rhine. We went through Beaumont, Letanne, Pouilly, Inor, with a night's rest at La Ferte. The next day saw us go through Marfut, cross into Belgium at Villers devant Orval, then to Gerouville and Bollefontaine to Tintigny. The next day through St. Marie, Etalle, Vance, Stockem, Arlon and a rest at Tantelange. The next day we went to Bissen, the next day to Ettulbruck, and now we are in a little village named Reisdorf.*

I doubt if you can find half these towns on your maps, but when I come home I'll bring my maps, trace out our course and tell you all about what happened at each place. This is really the most interesting trip that it is possible for anyone to make, and it will undoubtedly be history soon. Besides we have had some very pleasant surprises. In your last letter with the enclosed note from Dad, or rather in Dad's letter, he asks for me to bring home some relics. It is almost impossible for me to gather any relics and carry them around with me, for our baggage is very limited. All I have now is a Luger pistol, with a rather interesting little history, a boche map case with a couple of interesting maps, one of which I am using on this trip, and a belt buckle. I'll try from now on to gather up a little junk. But it is the boys in the SOS who have all the souvenirs from our men who are wounded and sent back to the hospitals. The worst of it is that these men will get all the credit. You will read in the papers that we are having turkeys and cranberries for Thanksgiving, but we get "monkey meat," and the people with soft jobs in Paris swipe all the turkeys. Thus it goes. We have never even seen a YMCA performance up here, yet the folks back home think that we get the benefit of their contributions. Please pardon the little tirade, but it's true.

My health still continues the best in the world, and I am really having the time of my life right now. But I'm getting homesick, and would give anything to be back home for Christmas and sit around with you forever and a day.

With lots of love,

Mac.

We stayed on the Meuse River for a few days and then started our march toward Germany. on November 17. We averaged 20 to 30 kilometers a day and made 42 kilometers one day, always marching under full arms and equipment. We had a million songs which we would sing on our interminable hikes. Some songs were old standards, while others were made up by the men, so musical talent was much appreciated in the company. I remember the first verse of one particular song, to the tune of "There was a Young Lady from Armentieres:"

> Johnny Lejeune went over to France, parlez-vous,
> He's got too much cloth in the seat of his pants,
> But he's got the best division in France,
> Rinky dinky parlez-vous.

MG. John A. Lejeune, USMC, our 2nd Division, AEF, Commander, had uniforms which did not fit him too well. As Ovid described him, "He walks like the hind legs of an elephant."

When we marched through the Grand Duchy of Luxembourg, the town of Ettlebruck met us with a five piece band, and several little girls dressed out in their best bib and tucker decorated Maj. Williams' horse with flowers. As we moved through the town, I became aware that a crowd of kids was tailing our company so I dropped back to see what was going on. Pvt. Wert "Tennessee" Hughes, USMCR, a colorful mountaineer school teacher in our unit, was a great craps shooter and you could tell when he was in funds because his leather tobacco sack, which he always kept around his neck, protruded noticeably. He evidently was in funds at this time and had lots of coins. Those French coins were not worth much to him, so "Tennessee" was taking out his coins and tossing them out to the crowd. All the kids were jumping on them, scrambling for the most.

We stopped in Ettlebruck and for the first time in all of our marches, we stayed in a good-sized hotel that had room for all the officers of the battalion. We got settled and set up our guard. We always set up an outpost, and if any stream was nearby, we would have a machine gun posted at a bridge crossing, even if just a foot bridge. One company would be assigned to set up the guard. We settled in this hotel, and Major Williams, Clif Cates, the battalion adjutant 1stLt. Lucian H. Vandoren, and I were having a repast in the dining room when in walked a towering figure, wearing an overcoat on the cold November day. We could see he was a U.S. Army general so we immediately jumped up and saluted. He looked at Maj. Williams, the senior officer, and demanded, "Where are your Co. offices?"

Williams replied, "We don't break out our offices on these one night stands, General." Angry, the General retorted, "Don't you realize that we're still in the state of war?"

"Yes, sir."

"Don't you think you should have your typewriters and your office staff here, all ready to handle business?"

Finally Maj. Williams got all red in the neck and said "Sir, I can tell by your uniform and the insignia that you are a general, but who are you?"

And he answered, "Young man, I'm your Corps Commander!"

He was Major General John L. Hines, Commanding General, 3rd U.S. Corps. Williams went out with him to inspect the galley and the other areas of our camp. The General bawled Williams out at every stop for picayune infractions, such as the mules not being properly curried. The next day Major Williams was relieved of command. He was gone only a couple of days and returned after someone at 2nd Division Headquarters put in a plea for him. But from that point on one inspector after another nosed around our outfit. They finally got Williams for not having an officer in command of a machine gun on the foot-bridge over a little creek and he was relieved of command of our battalion permanently. Major Williams' reputation was not hurt in the Marine Corps because an Army man had relieved him. So he got to go back home and did so with great glee. Maj. Williams was replaced by Maj. Franklin B. Garrett, USMC, who was an imposing figure but not very much of a character.

So we marched on toward Germany. We soon learned of the flu epidemic which hit the whole country. In one village we sent a billeting party out ahead to arrange a place for us to stay under cover. The party came back and reported three people dead in bed from the flu. We avoided that area and never had any flu at all, even in November and December. When I was recovering in the hospital I had heard the nurses talking about Spanish flu but I thought they were talking about Spanish fly.

As we marched, the weather was wonderful, even in December. I never had the least idea that it could be as mild as it was that far north. There was no snow whatever as yet, and while an overcoat was comfortable, it was not at all necessary. The country was beautiful too, there along the Rhine, and we found much more up-to-date towns along it than we were used to. The people we ignored as much as possible, but of course we lived in their houses, and we couldn't avoid contact. They were certainly well-trained by their own officers, and we got all sorts of service from them.

Our method of procedure when we entered a town was as follows. We sent ahead a man who could speak German, and he summoned the burgomaster and demanded that he be shown where all the available space was to house the men and animals. The houses found suitable were marked "so many men 78th Company." Then the people had to bring straw to the men to make their bunks on, and had to carry the wood and coal to heat the places. The officers of each company would find a good kitchen and put their orderlies and cook in charge. Then we were all set. The men's food was prepared in a rolling kitchen, which was nothing more than a receptacle for a lot of pots and kettles on wheels. When we moved every day, as we did for 9 straight days just before arriving at our destination, we finally got our billeting problem down to a system. We started that stretch with a twenty two mile hike and ended with a twenty mile one. The days in between, we never hiked less than seven or eight miles. We hiked over three hundred miles in all.

We kept on hiking until we crossed the Rhine River on Friday, December 13, and went upstream to the town of Rheinbrohl, Germany. The town, though small, supported a large factory and was an industrious little village. The only unpleasing feature was the occasional assault on our olfactory organs, due to the German method of gathering and spreading fertilizer. The "honey carts" were made the subject of an Army order. The order required that the carts had to be kept in a sanitary condition, although exactly how this could have been done without changing the entire function of the vehicle was beyond me. The German nose was evidently entirely out of order, and I believed they could live in perfect harmony with pole-cats.

We were very pleasantly situated in Rheinbrohl, and it initially was a great life over there among the square heads. At first we did not know how long we would remain there, but soon found that our battalion was set for occupation duty in the town. It was our first real rest, and chance to get cleaned up; besides, our routine was not nearly so tiring as we were used to. We drilled for two hours in the morning, had retreat in the afternoon, and the rest of our time was our own. The men were resourceful in their free time; we had venison and fried chicken for Christmas but the government didn't give it to us.

My work was not cut down however. I had all the office

work to supervise; I had to make out requisitions for clothing, equipment, and ordnance, much of which was lost or ruined during the continuous service in the field. But what I hated worst of all, every mail delivery brought me inquiries from bereft parents, many of which I was unable to answer satisfactorily. During our stay in France, more than a thousand names appeared on the rolls of the company; so because of our limited office equipment and the changes in the office, force records were much more incomplete than they should have been. But everything I was able to do, every scrap of information I could find, I sent home. It was especially difficult to write the father of Pvt. Robert C. Clore, 17th Co. (A), 5th Marine Regiment, a fine Wentworth graduate, who was killed at Belleau Wood. I learned from Bert Baston, the Minnesota football star who was a lieutenant in Bob's company, that Bob died as every good Marine would like to. His company had run into a nest of machine guns, and Bob was given the job of capturing one. He took four men and crawled up to within 75 yards of the machine gun. Then because there was no cover near, he thought it best to rush the gun. He went out ahead of his men firing his pistol, and he never let up until he was riddled with bullets. But he killed two of the Germans, and his men were able to capture the others on account of his sacrifice. Although Bob was not in my company, I was glad I could write Mr. Clore because I knew what it would mean to him.

We had no particular difficulty motivating the men to keep up the enthusiasm for drill and inspections after the Armistice. The men were antsy to get home, but they were disciplined, so no real trouble ever ensued. Of course a few court martials were unavoidable. I usually drilled my men in the morning, and in the afternoons we would be free to play football, baseball, or have some other recreation. I actually enjoyed drilling my four platoons with commands such as "On Right Into Line," "Squads Right," et al. I knew the drill movements from my

Wentworth days, and I think I can modestly say that I was a pretty fair drill master with a good command voice.

My company was still a source of great pride to me, although it frequently underwent changes. Five of the noncommissioned officers whom I recommended in November, were sworn in as officers a month later; so for a while I had 13 officers in the company. These promotions rather broke up the company organization, because I lost my best enlisted men; and newly made officers were never left with the companies from which they had been recommended. But I was mighty glad to see their worth recognized, and I think that their bars gained by their excellent work in the field, and under fire, meant more to them than if they were made from a school in the States. Of the company's officer's at the end of the war, 1stLt. Dale S. Young, USMC, and I were the only officers who did not come to France as enlisted men, and I was the only one who never served as a private in the Marine Corps.

Also in Rheinbrohl, with our battalion, there was a battalion of 12th U.S. Field Artillery Regiment, and I had a chance to make some friends among their officers. In our division there was the strongest feeling possible between the different branches of service. The Marines swore by the artillery and engineers, and vice-versa. We knew them by what they did with us and for us during our scraps, but there were no chances of becoming personally acquainted during the war. If an outsider knocked the Marines to our artillery there was at once a fight on, and the same was true with us. So we were indeed happy to meet each other. We got together and displayed mutual admiration and supreme contempt for all outsiders.

In the first week of January I attended a Division dance down at Neuwied. A number of nurses, Y.M.C.A., and Red Cross women workers were imported from Coblenz, and we had quite a gay time. There were so many Generals shaking a festive foot that I didn't have much of a show, also the floor was too jammed for comfort, but I enjoyed the crowd, and saw a few old friends. Ovid was there, but not dancing; so we chatted a while about home. The next break in our general routine came about a week later. Our schedule for drills in the Division called for an exhibition attack by a company in each regiment, and by some chance the job was assigned me. We had a long hike the day before it was due and I had no chance to rehearse as I wanted to. But my company was a good outfit; so I didn't fear the job. The Corps commander as well as Division commander were due to be present, but we seldom expected them unless something very important happened. So I was not surprised when they sent the Corps Inspector down instead, a Colonel. We "put his eye out" by our attack, and he said the performance was very credible.

The next day I was sent over as an umpire for a manoeuver in the 1st division. It was a most interesting trip, and I took advantage of the sidecar at my disposal, by traveling all over the area. The duties of umpiring were rather simple; so most of my time was taken in skylarking around. I went down through Neuwied, Engers, and up through Montabaum. I looked up an old classmate, Oscar Gates, whom I hadn't seen before over there. He appeared to have suffered no changes at all. I had dinner with him and we talked of the good old days at Wentworth. In all I enjoyed the trip immensely. Tommy Goodwin, my old Beta classmate who visited me in the hospital, also kept in touch with me. I tried to find him in my wanderings but he had acquired a job teaching school in Coblenz, so I missed him.

In mid-January I attended one of the nightly entertainments at the Hindenberg theatre. The program announced that the vaudeville artists of the 17th U.S. Field Artillery Regiment were to perform. So I was not surprised when Ovid came up to the officers' row. We sat together all evening and swapped experiences as usual. His gang had a very creditable show which we all enjoyed.

We kept active with the usual procedure of drilling. In the meantime, our battalion commander, Maj. Garrett, had been replaced by Major Edwin H. "Chief" Brainard, USMC, who was quite an officer. Brainard had never been in the line, but he was a "by the book" officer, and he checked gear carefully and looked under everything during inspections. Maj. Garrett had simply walked around and asked a question or two in his inspections. Maj. Brainard changed things considerably and set up a competitive inspection system. The 2nd Division also adopted a competition that was determined by inspections and drill. They would inspect our galley, our living quarters, and all other operations. Brainard got us in such good shape that our whole battalion made the honors list, whereas elsewhere only individual platoons or a company would be listed.

The competition ultimately became rather ridiculous. During one of our numerous parades, the Major and the adjutant of the battalion were mounted and received parade. Old Amos Shinkle had been promoted to company commander of the 79th Co. and was the senior officer at "Officers Front and Center." He forgot to give "Halt" until I ended up with my nose just about an inch from the commander's horse. To our disbelief, Shinkle was relieved of command for the infraction. Soon afterward, a captain named Basil Gordon was assigned to our battalion.

He was the stepson of the Commandant of the Marine Corps and had arrived in Europe after the Armistice. The incompetent Basil was shunted from one battalion to another, and he eventually was sent to ours. Maj. Brainard gave him the job of adjutant of the guard mount. The whole unit turned out to see how Basil would do in his new post. In a guard mount, the guard and the officer who was acting as adjutant would report to the officer of the day, who was behind him receiving the guard mount. Basil was acting as adjutant and got up to the point where he was to move the guard off the grounds. But he had the men at "Present Arms." Nobody ever moved when he was at "Present Arms." He gave the command, "At Trail, Platoons Right, March." Nobody moved, so he gave the command a second time with the same result. Finally he looked around at the officer of the day and said, "Captain, I don't believe they're going to do it."

At that time we also began to get numerous memoranda at company headquarters listing various opportunities for the men. One of these opportunities tempted me, seeking someone who qualified academically to go over to England to study at Cambridge or Oxford. Vandoren, the battalion adjutant, and I both wanted to go, but because we were making such a name for the battalion on inspections, Chief Brainard did not want to upset the applecart, and we were turned down. I really was not particularly anxious about the matter, because there was some faint chance of our being sent home before mid-summer, and of course I didn't care to miss that.

The post-war period had an interesting economic dimension also, for the German inflation was skyrocketing. I made the mistake of speculating in a few German marks, hoping I would make some money on my investment, but instead the marks were completely worthless in a short time. However, I did have a stroke of good fortune in early February when my trunk, bedding roll, and clothing bag, which I had lost after being wounded, turned up from the baggage department. I then had nearly everything I started out with. The only item I missed was a little manicure set my mother had given me. I was rather amused to find a few articles in my bedding roll which did not belong to me. Evidently someone carried it around awhile, lost it, and allowed it to stray back to my address.

In February, we were still having ideal snappy winter weather—real football weather. Some attention was being paid to athletics; so I had a chance of seeing some pretty good games. Our Division had an excellent team and in the tournament won the Corps Championship. They beat our old rivals the 1st Division and cleaned up on the 32nd Division. They also played the 4th Corps Champions at Coblenz. We were having a very strenuous schedule of training up here—a little too strenuous to suit us, and the Company & Battalion Commanders got the brunt of it. We received operation orders and had to tour the country simulating combat conditions with skeletonized units. Four men represented a company, but the commander had to be there. It was entirely an exercise for officers down to company commanders, and we had to ride 30 or 40 miles in an open truck—which in the winter weather was far from pleasant. Then too those Rhine hills were the steepest affairs I had ever climbed—they all reminded me of the descent from our old "look-out" to the "pump-house" in Lexington—and we had to cavort over them taking imaginary machine gun nests daily.

We were having considerable shifting of personnel in our battalion—officers were being detached to other organizations and there were more new jobs coming up than I could imagine. For a while I had thirteen officers in my company, and soon after I had hardly enough to drill the company. We also had a shifting of routine as we changed battalion commanders. We were indeed in an unsettled condition.

1stSgt. Frank A. Zettel, was a great help to me during this time. Zettel was not a typical first sergeant. He was a very mild little fellow who was a Certified Public Accountant. All the other company headquarters had the midnight oil burning, handling all the paperwork, while my company closed at 6 o'clock every night due to Zettel's efficiency. I signed everything he put in front of me without hesitation. One memo came through announcing that an A.E.F. tennis tournament was to be held and requested the names of any tennis players in the unit. So I told Zettel to send in my name and say that I was champion of Lafayette County, Missouri, but promptly forgot about it. He sent the form in, and in a couple of weeks I got orders to go to Cannes.

I went on a very fine trip down to the Mediterranean coast. Ostensibly the purpose of the trip was to participate in the tennis tournament, but I knew I had no chance as some of the best known American tennis players were there, and I was not much disappointed when I was thrown out in the first round. I did not even have tennis shoes. I was a pretty fair player, having beaten a member of the United States Davis Cup team while in college at Chicago, but I was no longer on top of my game. I had played a little tennis in the hospital back in Vichy to get back in physical condition, but I was not up to the competition. Our division did win the A.E.F. championship, since we had R. N. Williams who, though not a professional, was the best player in the United States at that time.

I was also privileged to watch Suzanne Lenglen, the premier woman tennis player in the world, play a few sets there. She looked like a horse but she could surely play tennis. I stayed in Cannes from February 17 to March 2 and met a couple of old Chicago fraternity brothers, John Baker and John Coulter. Cannes was a favorite old resort of King Edward's and was a half hours ride from Nice. Even though the latter place was better known at the time, Cannes was much more attractive.

But I had to return among the boches in early March. I couldn't say that I liked them any better on close acquaintance. An incident that happened after I returned from Cannes illustrated for me some of their characteristics. I was in one of these huge Army trucks returning from a manoeuver, and while we were coming through a village, a small German boy met us. He was riding a horse at the time, but when we came nearer, the horse threw him directly in front of our truck. We thought certainly that he would be killed or badly injured, but luckily all four wheels missed him. By the time we had stopped, his father had grabbed him and was pounding him over the head. They seemed to treat all their children in this manner, and it was not at all surprising to me that they grew up such beasts. I might have been prejudiced, but I didn't ever outgrow my condition.

While at Rheinbrohl, I had a billet in a house where a German man and his family lived. I did not talk to them, and they did not talk to me. We passed each other like ghosts. We really did not fraternize with any of the Germans. I never learned a word of German in all the time we were there. The only ones we talked with were the children, who kept saying they were going to get even with France eventually. The Germans were not really whipped, because their country had not been damaged physically, and they were a stubborn lot.

I do remember one amusing instance of fraternization, however. There was one lady who was not the best in the world. She was attractive but she, if you are familiar with your classics, was a sabine. Two men of my company were interested in her. One was a gunnery sergeant named GySgt. Harold E. Swanson, a very attractive fellow, and the other was 2ndLt. Edward C. Fowler, the former South Boston policeman and one of my platoon leaders. The girl preferred the gunnery sergeant, so Fowler wanted to bring charges against Swanson for giving food, vegetables, soap, and butter to a civilian. I certainly did not follow through on Fowler's complaints, and the crisis soon subsided.

During the month of March I received orders to take my company out to build a rifle range. We found a suitable spot in the surrounding hills above the Rhine and constructed a range. Some of the boys killed deer and we had venison. I thought I would like to get a deer once, so I went up and sat awhile. One deer sprinted by at full speed, and I missed him by 10 yards. I was disgusted with my poor shooting and did no more hunting.

Maj. Brainard was such a humdinger of a battalion commander that we were always busy in a constructive way. We schemed all the time on the best way to make the men comfortable and efficient, and of course there was much to be done along this line. The most important job for us was the problem of food. We drew a good ration, but our problem was to prepare and serve it well. We had to resort to every means to get things going. I had a big company fund when I took command. While troops were in a barracks, the company drew so much money per man per day. Consequently much could be saved. But when troops were in the field, so much actual food was issued. With the company fund we were able to buy dishes and all the fixings.

The 2nd Engineer Regiment built us a mess hall and we fitted it up with tables, a cement floor, an oven which one of my corporals constructed, sanitary meat safes, flour bins and all sorts of stuff. The medical authorities inspected daily and graded all these kitchens. At first they came down to criticize, but then they came to show us off. Our battalion had the reputation of having the best kitchens in the Army. We scouted up paint for the tables—a sky blue was the only color to be found —and my mess officer commandeered a bunch of large potted plants, and small ones for the tables. The men entered into the spirit of the competition, and the stories we heard of the Army outfits not being able to get stuff merely offered added incentive to our efforts.

Our drill schedule was not too strenuous through April and May. We had three hours in the morning while the afternoon was devoted to athletics. We had a baseball game every good afternoon. And when we were not playing ourselves, we went to the bigger games between the 2nd and 3rd division teams, and since there was bitter feeling between the two outfits, they turned out to be fine exhibitions. The game that sticks in my mind was one we lost 2 to 1.

On one occasion, the regiment had a picnic, and we somehow commandeered a steamship. We invited some American nurses and telephone operators to share the occasion, and we took the boat up the Rhine along with our engineers. As part of the outing, the 2nd Engineer Regiment built a pontoon bridge across the Rhine River. Incidentally, it was near that very spot where the Remagen Bridge was built then later captured during World War II by my Wentworth classmate General Bill Hoge. We had quite a time on the steamship. I was in demand because I played the piano a little bit. We sang songs and had a fine time.

Ovid's regiment, the 17th U.S. Field Artillery Regiment, was upstream from us in the town of Bendorf, Germany and I visited him there. His commanding officer was quite a character who had some trouble with his men getting "spiritus fermenti." He talked to the mayor of the town and demanded that he put a stop to the flow of alcohol. When the mayor was unsuccessful in doing so, he was called in and the commander had the regimental surgeon give him a physical examination. The doctor reported that he was very sound in limb and body, so the commander had him taken down and dumped in the icy Rhine. The supply of alcohol to Ovid's unit withered after that incident. Shortly after that the 17th U.S. Field Artillery Regiment was moved to Coblenz, the 2nd Division, AEF, center.

I visited Ovid at Coblenz a number of times. A very ancient castle called Ehrenbreitstein stood on a bluff across the river from Coblenz. On one occasion we gathered quite a supply of different colored combat flares that had been used to indicate that we were going to advance, that we were gassed, that we were held up, etc. A group of us climbed up the bluff, and we shot off a whole bunch of those flares. I have forgotten what the occasion was, but it made quite a sight with the flares bursting above the castle, kind of a miniature Fourth of July celebration.

I had another memorable experience when a small group of us took an outfit's Stanley Steamer up a road to an area where we had no business being, since we Americans were restricted to a semicircular area around our occupation area, just as were the French and the British. But we went beyond that, up the river, and arrived at a very attractive looking hotel. The hotel owner, who also happened to be a wine merchant, came out and asked whether we would like a little American whiskey. We did not object, and we had quite a visit with him. We could have been in trouble if we had been discovered, but we were not.

The first week of May, I wanted to see my brother Sandy. I

was afraid his division would shove out before I got a chance to see him; so I had to apply for a pass. I got a short leave and went to Mainz where his company was located and had a visit with him. Sandy looked as fit as a fiddle and was enjoying the prospect of getting home. My father also had to undergo an operation that spring, and the slowness of the mail caused me a good deal of anxiety over his well-being. But I finally received a letter from home giving me the news that Dad had recovered nicely. I never really allowed myself to worry much, because I had seen so much abnormal surgery which was so successful that I had lost all dread of the knife. But nevertheless it was a great relief to be positive that Dad was well.

I was becoming resigned to staying in Germany. We had steel double decker bunks for all the men, passes were given out freely to everyone, we were eating excellent food, getting plenty of exercise, had enough to do to keep us busy, were saving our money, and in addition the weather had cleared up wonderfully. The leaves were out on all the trees and the orchards were a mass of blooms. The date of our return was still a matter of wild conjecture; one minute it looked as if we were to go home early in June and the next, we were to be sent to the Balkans or Russia. The rumor most prevailing was that the 1st and 2nd Divisions, AEF, would be the last to leave. But even at that it hardly seemed possible that we would be kept longer than a couple of months more.

We were finally ordered back to the United States after eight months in Germany. From July 19th to the 21st of 1919, I took one of the most pleasant train rides I have ever had on the famous *40 Hommes, 8 Chevaux* to the French coastline. I had my carpenter fix a few big wooden stands to serve as tables, because the cars we were in had two seats facing each other with nothing between. We could set the stands up and have meals on them, play cards on them, or put our bedding rolls on them for a little rest. We strolled along at such an unhurried pace that we hardly ever caught up with the smoke from the engine in front until we reached Brest. The man in charge there was the legendary BG. Smedley Darlington Butler, USMC. He ran Brest extremely well. The messes were excellent. Wooden walks were everywhere to keep us out of the mud, and he saw that we got new uniforms. Before our departure we were given very thorough physical examinations, and out of our battalion of 1000 men, only five were not allowed to board the ship. This statistic is a true testament to how rare fraternization actually was. One of the men had gonorrhea, another had syphilis, and three had scabies, an infectious skin disease.

After embarking on the U.S.S. *George Washington* in the afternoon of Monday, July 28, 1919, we Marines were supposed to take part in the management of the ship. Maj. Brainard was given the job of Berthing and Spacing Officer. But Brainard was a sea lawyer and he had no intentions of doing any work coming back on the ship, so he did some investigating and found that my job as Policing Officer was senior to his position. Not surprisingly, I soon found myself as Berthing and Spacing Officer. I was thereafter required to accompany the ship's captain on his inspection early every morning, and I had to assign lieutenants to "Officer on Duty" posts. There were 16 compartments below deck, and an officer had to be on duty 24 hours a day in each one of those compartments. Over a hundred lieutenants were given to me for my assignments. After I made up a schedule and got my orders out for the Berthing and Spacing Officers, I did not have very much to do other than inspect the ship with the captain every morning. The men slept in compartments with their bunks right on top of each other, four or five high. A large group of brides sailed with us, but they were not allowed to be with their husbands during the trip. Four or five of these young ladies occupied each stateroom.

We landed at the AEF Port of Debarkation at Hoboken, New Jersey on the morning of Sunday, August 3, and traveled by train to Camp Mills, New York that was on Long Island. On

August 8, we paraded in New York City's streets. We marched down Fifth Avenue from 125th Street down to Wall Street and the Battery, but by that time the bloom was off the peach, and the parade was no ticker tape affair. The war had been over too long at that point. The whole 4th Brigade (Marine) then boarded trains and headed back to Marine Barracks, Quantico, Virginia and then to Washington D.C. for a parade down Pennsylvania Avenue on Tuesday, August 12.

We arrived in Washington D.C. fairly early in the morning. I wandered around a little bit, and some Marines were engaged in a big crapshooting game in the entrance to one of the Congressional Office Buildings. A congressman came out to watch us and said, "Well, if it wasn't so public I'd like to join you." He did not bother us at all. Wherever the boys were, they had a crap game going on. Evidently a lot of crap shooting and gambling games were played aboard the return ship, and one fellow supposedly won about $15,000. I do not know whether that was the case, but it very probably could be, because a lot of the money gravitated to a very few. At any rate we marched well in Washington, and I recall doing an "Eyes Left" toward President Wilson.

That parade wrapped things up except for the red tape of discharging all the men, although a few career noncoms remained in the service. The day the outfit broke up, Wednesday, August 13, 1919, my boys gave me a beautiful Hamilton gold pocket watch with the Marine Corps emblem on one side and the 6th Regiment insignia on the other. Inside the case it was inscribed: "To our skipper from the boys of the 78th." It is one of my most prized possessions.

11

RECRUITING DUTY

After the 78th disbanded, I rushed back home to Lexington with 30 days leave. While at home, I received orders to go to Spokane, Washington on recruiting duty. After I left Kansas City in mid-September of 1919, I had a most interesting, though tedious trip through Nebraska, a corner of Wyoming, Montana, Idaho and finally into Washington to Spokane. The funniest thing that happened was when we came through Lincoln. I happened to think about friends, the Buntings, living there, and the first people I saw at the station were Gladys Bunting and her two children. We had an hour's delay, and I got out and talked to them until Gladys' husband Arch came in on a train from Omaha. Their daughter, Ann, and I once had a terrible crush on each other, and Gladys insisted that I stay there and visit them. They had a new enclosed Dodge car, and it was somewhat of a temptation to linger, but orders is orders and it couldn't be considered.

The eastern part of Montana was as dry as a bone all that summer, and it was the most desolate, bare, hopeless, parched land I had ever seen. An occasional homesteader's cabin was about the only evidence of civilization we could see, and where the occupant got his water was a mystery to me. Natives of this country said that thousands of cattle had to be shipped out of the country to other states in order to find grazing land for them.

I met two other young traveling men who were connected with the Winchester Small Arms and Ammunition Company, who were busy making rifles and ammunition for the Army during the late unpleasantness. One of them spotted my Phi Beta Kappa key, and since he was a college man, started the conversation. At Billings one of the former corporals in my Company boarded the train, and we chewed the rag the rest of the trip to Spokane. So I did not lack for company on the trip.

After I got to Spokane about 8:15 p.m., I went up to the leading hotel, the Davenport, and tried to get a room. There were no single rooms left, but there were some double rooms available, and an old respectable looking man was in the same fix that I was; so we doubled up. He was a United Presbyterian preacher who had come to Spokane to attend a synod meeting. I found he was one of the most interesting talkers I ever met, and we talked for several hours. He told me a lot of his experiences in dealing with misunderstandings in his congregation, when he was a youngster and had taken over his first charge. He had been pastor in a wealthy suburb of Pittsburgh, and he had held the same church for twenty years. I told him a few of my experiences, but by far the most of the conversation was carried on by him.

I reported to the Spokane office as soon as I arrived to find out what I could. There was a Lieutenant on the job, an old timer who had been twenty-two years in the services. He had received his commission after the war broke out, but now that the decrease in the Marines had gone through, he had to become a first sergeant again. I thought it was an awful shame for an old fellow like him, married too as he was, to be reduced in rank like that.

My job consisted mainly in awaiting recruits and swearing them in. It was a very slack season as I well imagined, and the boys were not falling over themselves to get in. But we got a few every now and then. There were seven stations in Montana, or rather in the Montana district. One was in Wyoming, and my one was of course in Washington. There were one or two sergeants in the outlying stations, but all their recruits came through my office. I made a tour of my district the first of October to get acquainted with them. The work was quite different from anything I had ever done, and I felt like a green horn on the job. But my first sergeant was pretty well up on everything, and I had to rely on him.

I did not have time to become acquainted much with Spokane in those first few weeks. But we had a fine set of offices there, right on the main street on a well-lighted corner of the second floor. I could look out and see all the traffic, which was about the sum and substance of my duties. The weather was too fine and the jobs were too plentiful to make recruits plentiful; so we waited for the cold weather to drive the men in from the ranches. Spokane seemed to be a mighty clean town, progressive, with an excellent residential district. The people were a fine looking, rugged, healthy looking lot and I initially had no doubt that I would like it there.

On the 6th and 7th of October, I got orders to go to Nezperce, Idaho to investigate a case of a man whose discharge had been requested. As far as convenience went, it was one of the worst trips I ever took, but there was some pretty fine scenery along our route. I had to take the trip during the daytime both ways, and it was necessary to change cars twice on each trip. The first lap was from Spokane to Lewistown, where it was necessary to change for Vollmer, Idaho. At Vollmer I had to take a private line, owned and operated by some farmers down in that section of the country. The pretty part of the trip was from Lewistown to Vollmer. We started out at the bottom of a canyon and gradually worked up along it's sides till we came out at the bottom of a plateau. It was the steepest country that I had ever seen, and I thought that it constituted a good prelude to a visit to the Grand Canyon. The private owned road was typical of the slow train through Arkansas variety. It consisted of an antiquated engine and one combination passenger and baggage car. The train had to slow down almost to a stop about six times in order for the brakeman to get off and scare cattle off of the tracks. There were six so-called stations on the line, and people would get off and on at them, and disappear over the hills, but there were no houses anywhere to be seen. About half of the passengers were Indians. I was told that they were Lapways. They were fat, greasy and very good natured, and invariably spoke their own dialect. The men never spoke any English at all; in case it was necessary to do some talking with white people, the squaws did all the translating.

My business was transacted in about fifteen minutes after I arrived at the town of Nezperce; and I went out to look over the town. There were some 500 inhabitants, but I think the census was stuffed. I found a couple of lads who had been in the 2nd U.S. Engineer Regiment with our division, and I had quite a chat with them down in the pool-hall, which was the only place open at the time.

I also received orders in October to take an examination in Seattle to determine my permanent lineal rank in the Marine Corps. This did not mean that I might be made a Major-General, or if I fell down that I should be made a Second Lieutenant, but simply it meant that my rank would be determined with respect to the other members of my class, those who came in as officers at the same time that I did. I did not have more than half of the books that I was supposed to take the examination on and I had to borrow them from various places in order to have any idea of the subjects. So when I went up for the exam, I had an idea, but that was about all, of the various subjects; there were eleven of them, and I was supposed to have mastered several large books in connection with each one.

Naturally I did not look forward to the trial with any degree of confidence.

The exams took place on October 14 to 17 inclusive. For my own self-respect more than anything else I studied pretty hard from the time I received notice that they were to be held, and I did not take time off even for correspondence. My trip to Seattle was rather unexciting. As soon as I arrived, I had to cross the Sound and go over to Marine Barracks at the Navy Yard, where the examinations were to be held. I arrived at night, and the trip over the Sound the next morning was through a fog so dense that I could see nothing. When I arrived at the Marine Barracks, I found that a couple of my old friends in the Officers School at Quantico were there. Neither had crossed over to France, and I had forgotten their names. But it was good to see a familiar face anyhow. The Major who oversaw the exams was on the board which passed on us in Chicago when I first came in. Our first exam started about fifteen minutes after I arrived, and the following afternoons and mornings were similarly taken up, until the 17th of October when I started back to Spokane.

A former lieutenant in the Marine Corps came up to see me after I returned to Spokane, and he suggested that I go over to the University Club, and meet a few friends of his. I did so and found that I was eligible for an economical service membership; so I put in my application and joined the Club. In this way I hoped to meet quite a few of the Spokane elite in order to make my stay there more pleasant.

I settled down to conditions pretty well by late October, and I found a couple of very good friends with whom most of my time was taken up. One was Dr. Joses, a Naval Physician who was attached to the recruiting District as medical examiner. He was married, and he stayed in the same family hotel with me, the Alexandria, it was called, and we spent a great number of our evenings there playing chess while his wife was visiting her parents in San Francisco. He learned the game during the war while on board one of the transports, and was really quite good. I was glad to be able to revive my interest in the game. The other friend was another doctor, Farley by name. He was about six feet four in height, and weighed well over two hundred. He looked exactly like the famous movie actor, Fatty Arbuckle, if the latter were trained down to good proportions. His family which consisted of a wife and four children was also visiting with relatives in the East; so he was another member of our chess club. I had a couple of dinners at his home, which he had sublet to a minister and his family. Farley looked rather young to be such a family man, but he was a prince of a fellow, and a man of high ideals. He was superintendent of the Congregationalist Sunday School, and I had thought about attending his church. There was a Methodist church just a block from me, but there were no Presbyterian churches anywhere near. So I had difficulty deciding on exactly which church would be best for me to identify myself with.

I made a few ventures into society. The first was when I stepped out to the movies with a young man whom I met through an ex-Marine officer, and a couple of girls. They were distinctly of the elite of Spokane, the young man being an ex-student of Yale, and the young lady who was with me, the daughter of one of the wealthiest men in town. She had been in Dresden when the war broke out; but in spite of her wide travels, she did not appear to be of exceptional brain capacity. After the movies we enjoyed a little dancing at the Davenport Hotel. As we were returning from the dance, it was snowing, and the streets were all wet, but it was not very cold. The streets were slick, and the autos of the day did considerable skidding; our car, on making a turn, skidded all the way around, and started in the opposite direction. Luckily, although the car was a large one, we missed the curb.

The recruiting work proceeded satisfactorily through October, though not quite as well as it might have been. Our physical examinations were so strict that it was necessary to reject a very large percentage of our applicants. These we sent over to the Army, where they were welcomed with open arms. But the result was that our figures were not very high. I was also disappointed when I learned that I had to miss the big reunion scheduled for the 2nd Division in December.

By the middle of December I was bored stiff and submitted my resignation. While I was waiting to hear from Washington, I thought it advisable to have my nose fixed up a bit; so a very good Doctor performed what is known as a submucous resection on me, and took a lot of bone, thus straightening out the air passages through my nostrils. The result would be to alleviate quite a bit my tendency to catch cold, sniffle, and cough. I was not being particularly bothered at the time, in fact I hadn't had a cold since I had been up here. But I believed that such a time was best to have such a job performed; so I did it without informing any of my family to spare them worry.

On the morning of Friday, December 19, I received a notice that my resignation had been favorably acted upon, and that as soon as a relief was provided I would get my walking papers. For a time when there appeared to be prospects for trouble in Mexico, I almost sent in a cancellation of my request for discharge. But circumstances changed and everything pointed to a continuance of the old pussyfooting policy of letting the Mexicans get away with everything. So I thought I might as well get out and remain peaceful for the rest of my life. I sometimes wished that I had put in a request to go to China or some other place more interesting, but I spent six boring months in Spokane.

I received advice directly from Headquarters, Marine Corps, Washington D.C., stating that I was to be relieved on Friday, January 30, 1920 but I received no further word until my relief turned up almost a full month later. I could not imagine anything more unsatisfactory, as I was eager to get back to Wentworth and my family. I hoped my brother Sandy, now serving as Wentworth's superintendent, had a lot of work saved up for me as he promised, because I had a lot of energy stored up which hadn't had a chance to get an outlet for some time. About the only exercise I could take in Spokane was to walk, and I could do that for a long time without feeling as though I had taken a work out. I looked forward to getting out the boxing gloves and punching my brother in the nose. My relief finally arrived the morning of Monday, February 23, 1920 and thus ended my active duty in the Marine Corps.

APPENDIX

LOG OF THE 2ND BATTALION, 6TH REGIMENT, 4TH BRIGADE (MARINE), 2ND DIVISION

American Expeditionary Forces Record
1918 - 1919

(From the papers of James McBrayer Sellers.)

This log evidently was kept to give the location of the 2nd Battalion. It could then be referred to in order to find where they had been on any past date. Whether in the front line, support, reserve, or a training area, a unit's location was always noted in its relationship to the front. However, this log gives only faint idea as to the rugged fighting, heavy losses sustained, distance advanced, or the large numbers of prisoners captured. Gas was mentioned only twice while gas attacks were in reality numerous; the 96th Co. at Belleau Wood was nearly 100 percent evacuated to the hospital as gas casualties.

This log tells very briefly the part the 2nd Battalion, 6th Regiment, U. S. Marines took in the A.E.F. as a fighting unit of the 2nd Division, AEF. Records show that the 2nd Division advanced more kilometers against the enemy, and captured more prisoners and more equipment than any other Division of the A.E.F. In killed and wounded unfortunately the 2nd was also at the top. Without counting the 1st Division, AEF, the losses were one half of the total A.E.F. losses. The 1st Division losses were almost as great as that of the 2nd, and only the 1st Division spent a greater number of days at the front.

The 2nd Battalion, 6th Marines formed at Marine Barracks, Quantico, Virginia, on July 14, 1917. Two trains of 14 coaches each, full of Marines arrived from Marine Barracks, Mare Island, California; some units were brought up from Marine Barracks, Paris Island, others from Marine Barracks, League Island, Philadelphia Navy Yard and from other points on the East Coast. Among those to arrive were many old non-coms with four or five hash marks who had seen action in the Philippines, the Boxer Rebellion, and other troubled spots around the world. Major Thomas Holcomb was the Battalion Commander and later moved to the top of the Marine Corps. The Battalion trained seven months before going overseas as part of the 2nd Division, AEF. All other units of the 2nd had preceded Holcomb's Battalion to France, by several months, when they set sail on January 16 from Philadelphia Navy Yard and landed at St. Nazaire, France, Tuesday, February 5, 1918.

The following is from the official log of the 2nd Battalion, 6th Regiment, 2nd Division, A.E.F.

February, 1918

1-5 On board U.S.S. *Henderson* at sea.

    5 - Arrived at Base Section #1.

    8 - Disembarked St. Nazaire, France.

    8-11 - Enroute by rail to destination at training area.

    12-28 - Billeted at Robecourt in intensive training preparatory for front line service.

March, 1918

1-16 - Continued training at Robecourt and readying for move to the front.

17-18 - By rail and march to front area. (At this time we [2nd Division] had information of being part of the French 1st Army Corps.)

19 - In reserve at Camp at Massa and held there as reserves.

19-27 - In reserve in camp at Massa.

28 - Moved into front; engaged enemy at Bonzai, Toulon Sector, Verdun Front.

29-31 - Entrenched front line at Bonzai.

April, 1918

1 - Entrenched at Bonzai. Repulsed enemy attack.

2-7 - At Bonzai night raids made. Night raids repulsed.

9-17 - Moved back to reserve near Marquenteere.

18 - Changed by night to new station at Camp Chifoure in reserve.

19-21 - Moved up and in support near Chifoure.

22 - Shifted to support at Camp Romaine.

23-24 - Camp Renvon in reserve.

25-29 - At Camp Romaine reserve.

30 - Enroute by march to Watronville.

May, 1918 - Verdun

1-3 - In reserve near town of Watronville.

4 - Moved to front and engaged enemy in front of Watronville and entrenched.

5-11 - Entrenched near Watronville. Enemy raids repulsed.

12 - Relieved from front trenches by march to Chaney.

13-20 At training area Chaney, France.

21-22 - Enroute by rail to Serans Training area.

23-30 - In training area at Serans.

31 - Enroute all night and day by Camion into evening dark. After short rest moved up into support of retreating French troops in Belleau Woods, Chateau-Thierry area.

June, 1918 – Battle of the Aisne (Belleau Wood)

1 - Into immediate action stopping early morning attack by enemy and repeated afternoon and evening attacks. (Advance of enemy was now stopped—kilometers from Paris after complete rout of French troops who were having been driven back 5 kilometers a day for several days.)

1-5 - Entrenched near Triangle Farm resisting one and two attacks by enemy daily.

6 - Attack on enemy. Vicious resistance. Heavy losses sustained. Heavy losses inflicted. Day's advance 5 kilometers and town of Bouresche captured. Casualties heavy, companies reduced 50 to 70%.

7 - Resisted heavy evening dusk counter attack. Inflicted heavy casualties to enemy.

8 - Improving entrenchment at Bouresche resisting another vicious attack.

9-10 - Counter attacks resisted with less difficulty. Receiving heavy shelling continuously from enemy. Some gas shelling with casualties.

11 - Relieved and retired to reserve in woods near Montrieul.

12 - At Montrieul.

13 - Moved up relieved front troops.

14 - Early morning attack into Belleau Woods advance 5 kilometers - entrenched.

15 - Advanced 5 kilometers into heavy resistance. Entrenched near town of Lucy la Bocage.

16 - Relieved moved back to reserve in woods near Montrieul.

17-25 - Reserve Montrieul.

25 - Moved back to reserve in Soisson area.

26-30 - In reserve Soisson area.

31 - Enroute by rail changing station to Chavigny, France.

July, 1918 – Belleau Wood, Aisne-Marne Offensive (Soissons)

1-5 - Entrenched in front line at hill 142. Heavy artillery exchange. Gas shells from enemy with casualties daily.

6 - Moved back after relief to woods near Paris Metz Road.

7-9 - Bivouacked in woods near Paris Metz Road.

10 - Moved up to support of heavy action near town of Bezu.

11-14 - In support near Bezu.

15-16 - In support of action in capture of town of Nantuil.

17-18 - Moved back and by camion and march to Soisson area and moved up to front ready to attack.

19-24 - Attack and advance several kilometers to near Vierzy Soissons. Strong resistance and quite heavy casualties.

25 - Moved back to reserve in Soisson area.

26-30 - In reserve Soisson area.

31 - Enroute by rail changing station to Chavigny, France.

August, 1918 – Marbache Sector

1-4 - In Billets at Chavigny.

5-6 - Night marches changing station to Pontamousson.

7 - Into front line at trenches Pontamousson.

8 - Attack and advance.

9 - Attack and advance strong resistance.

10-11 - Entrenched counter attacks made and resisted.

12-17 - Entrenched Pontamousson area; Artillery duelling and less determined attacks by enemy resisted.

18 - Relieved from front trenches moved back to Camp Bois de L'evecque.

19-20 - Reserve Bois de L'evecque.

21 - Enroute by march changing station.

22-31 - In billets at Autrieville.

September, 1918 – St. Mihiel Offensive

1-2 - In billets at Autrieville.

2-11 - In night marches through Bois de Thuilly, Chaudeney, St. Geangolt and Manon Court.

12 - Into front lines and immediate attack and advance to capture Thiaucourt.

13-14 - Advanced to capture Bois de la Montague, St. Mihiel Sector.

15-16 - Entrenched front line near St. Mihiel.

17-21 - St. Mihiel front trenches.

21 - Relieved and moved back.

21-26 - Changing station night marches to Charmes Les Cotes.

27-29 - In billets at Sarry.

30 - By camion changing station to Suippe, Champagne Sector.

October, 1918 – The Battle of Blanc Mont Ridge

1 - In reserve trenches near Suippes.

2 - Moved into support trnches near Blanc Mont Ridge.

3 - Attack and capture of Blanc Mont Ridge, Vicious resistance.

4 - Relieved front trenches moved into support trenches Blanc Mont Ridge.

5 - Moved up launched attack and advanced two kilometers past Blanc Mont Ridge.

6 - Moved back to reserve near Suippe.

7-9 - Reserve near Suippe.

10 - Moved back to barracks at Camp Nantivet

11-12 - At Nantivet.

13 - Moved by march to training area at Laverne, France.

14-20 - At Laverne.

21 - Returned to Nantivet.

22 - Night march to Leffencourt.

23 - In billets at Leffencourt.

24 - Night march.

25 - En route by Camion.

26 - By march arrived Meusse-Argonne area.

27-29 In reserve in Argonne.

30 - Moved up formed a front line to start early morning attack and advance.

November, 1918 – The Meuse-Argonne Offensive, "Long March"

1 - Early morning attack behind rolling barrage eight or nine kilometers advance before entrenching in Argonne Woods.

2 - Attack and Advance.

3 - Attack and Advance.

4 - Attack and advance five to seven kilometers daily advance against heavy rear guard action of retreating German troops. Many prisoners and equipment captured.

5 - Night relief and to reserve in woods.

6-8 - Reserve in woods.

9 - Moved up to front.

10 - Attack and swift advance to near Meuse River.

11 - Early A.M. attack and advance across Meuse River and entrenched all shelling and firing stopped 11 a.m. - Armistice in effect.

12-14 - Bivouacked in woods near Yoncq.

15-16 - Bivouacked in woods near Besasce.

17 - Moved to Beaumont and started march to Rhine.

18 - Marching entered Belgium.

19 - March - night at Willers.

20 - Marching billeted at Tontelange.

21 - Entered Luxembourg.

22 - Marching billeted Ettlebruck.

23 - Marched to and billeted at Reisdorf, Luxembourg to be held here to await first of December agreed date to enter Germany.

23-30 - Billeted at Reisdorf.

December, 1918 – 3rd U.S. Army Occupation of the Koblenz Bridgehead, Germany

1 - Entered Germany via Wallendorf billeted Emmelbaum.

2 - Marched to and billeted at Pintesfiel.

3 - To Washeid and billeted.

4 - To Weinsheim and billeted.

5 - To Hillisheim and billeted.

6 - To Dollendorf and billeted.

7 - To Winneraf and billeted.

8 - To Nevenahr and billeted.

9 - Marched to Brohl on the Rhine and billeted.

10-12 - At Brohl in billets.

13 (Friday) - Crossed the Rhine River by ferry Hindenburg, to Rheinbrohl, Germany, establishing 2nd Division Army of Occupation.

13-31 - Army of Occupation at Rheinbrohl.

January, 1919

Army of Occupation at Rheinbrohl.

February, 1919

Army of Occupation at Rheinbrohl.

March, 1919

Army of Occupation at Rheinbrohl.

April, 1919

Army of Occupation at Rheinbrohl.

May, 1919

Army of Occupation at Rheinbrohl.

June, 1919

1-17 - Army of Occupation at Rheinbrohl.

18 - Marched from Rheinbrohl to Bonnesville and bivouacked in woods.

19 - Marched to Hershbach where a front line for action formed. Troops were ready to advance. (Troops were moved into the Buffer Zone at this time to put pressure on signing of peace terms which had been agreed upon to be by July 1.)

19-28 - Maintained line at Hershbach.

29 - Peace terms reported signed and march back started and bivouacked for night at Gladbach in woods.

30 - Arrived back at Rheinbrohl. Reoccupied old billets left June 18.

July, 1919 - Home

1-18 - Army of occupation Rheinbrohl, Germany.

19 - Entrained for Brest, France for voyage back to United States.

20 - Enroute by train through Belgium into France.

21 - Arrived Brest billeted in barracks.

21-27 - Readying for return voyage to United States.

28 - Embarked U.S.S. *George Washington*.

29-31 - At sea.

August, 1919 – Marine Barracks, Quantico, VA, Deactivation

1-3 - At sea.

3 - Arrived and disembarked at Hoboken.

4 - By rail to Camp Mills, Long Island.

5-6 - Camp Mills.

7 - Parade New York City and back to Camp Mills.

9 - By train to Quantico.

11-13 - At Quantico - Mustered out August 13, 1919.

PHOTOGRAPHS

TO SEE THESE PHOTOGRAPHS IN A COLORIZED
FORM, PLEASE VISIT THE FACEBOOK PAGE "C'EST LA
GUERRE"

James McB. Sellers during his time at Wentworth Military Academy

Left to Right, 1st Lt. Ovid R. Sellers, Chaplain Corps, USAR, Regimental Headquarters, 17th U.S. Field Artillery Regiment, 2nd Field Artillery Brigade, 2nd Division, AEF, Capt. Sandford Sellers Jr., USAR, Commanding Officer, Co C. 342nd Machine Gun Battalion, 178th Brigade, 89th Division, AEF, Capt. James McB. Sellers, USMC, Commanding Officer, 78th Co (E). 6th Marine Regiment, 4th Brigade (Marine), 2nd Division, AEF

From left to right, Capt. James McB. Sellers, USMC, Commanding Officer, 78th Co (E). and 1st Lt. James P. Adams, USMC, Executive Officer, 78th Co (E) near the German town of Rheinbrohl, Germany

2nd Lt. (former GySgt.), Robert C. Fowler, USMCR, 78th Co
(E). & 96th Co (H). 6th Marine Regiment

Family photograph taken after their return from Europe at
the family home in Lexington, Missouri. Left to Right, Capt.
Sandford "Sandy" Sellers, Jr., USAR (brother), Lucia
Valentine Rogers Sellers (mother), Capt. James McBrayer
Sellers, USMC, Sandford Sellers (father), Pauline Sellers
Richardson (sister), 1st Lt. Ovid Roger Sellers, USA (brother)

Capt. James McBrayer Sellers, USMC. and the Officers
(Company Executive Officer, and Platoon Commanders) of
78th Company (E). 6th Marine Regiment

Pvt. John J. Kelly, 78th Co (E). 6th Marine Regiment. Awarded the Medal of Honor (Army & Navy), Silver Star Medal, French Médaille Militaire, French Croix de Guerre w/Palm & Bronze Star, Italian War Cross for Military Valor, and Montenegrin Silver Medal for Valor for his actions while serving as an Company Runner with the 78th Co (E). during the 2nd Battalion, 6th Marine Regiment's attack on fixed enemy positions while on the summit of the Blanc Mont Massif (Hill 210) during The Battle of Blanc Mont Ridge on the morning of Thursday, October 3rd, 1918

Cpl. John H. Pruitt, 78th Co (E). 6th Marine Regiment. Awarded the Medal of Honor (Army & Navy), Silver Star Medal, Purple Heart Medal, French Croix de Guerre w/Gilt Star, Italian War Cross for Military Valor, and Montenegrin Silver Medal for Valor for his actions while serving as an Squad Leader with the 78th Co (E). during the 2nd Battalion, 6th Marine Regiment's attack on fixed enemy positions while on the summit of the Blanc Mont Massif (Hill 210) during The Battle of Blanc Mont Ridge on the morning of Thursday, October 3rd, 1918.

Capt. Robert E. Messersmith, USMC, Commanding Officer,
78th Company (E). 6th Marine Regiment, and future
Battalion Commander, 2nd Battalion, 5th Marine Regiment.

Photograph taken of Captain James McBrayer Sellers,
USMC. Commanding Officer, 78th Company (E). 6th Marine
Regiment after being awarded the Army Distinguished
Service Cross for his actions during the Battle of the Aisne,
(Belleau Wood) on the evening of Thursday, June 6th, 1918

ABOUT GRAY SPARROW BOOKS

Sparrows are the humblest of birds. They represent the common person. We can't all soar like eagles or strut like peacocks.

Gray Sparrow Books seeks to give a voice to the humblest among us who have a message for the world. We think *everyone* should be able to hear from these thought leaders, storytellers, practitioners. We want to share their wisdom so we all can learn and grow.

Here's to these birds, these people, these ideas.

Also by Gray Sparrow Books:

Fantastic Voyage: A Story School Turnaround and Achievement

The Best Game: A Simple and Memorable Model for Running Any Organization